John Dewey

THEORY FOR A GLOBAL AGE

Series Editor: Gurminder K. Bhambra

Globalization is widely viewed as a current condition of the world, but there is little engagement with how this changes the way we understand it. *The Theory for a Global Age* series addresses the impact of globalization on the social sciences and humanities. Each title will focus on a particular theoretical issue or topic of empirical controversy and debate, addressing theory in a more global and interconnected manner. With contributions from scholars across the globe, the series will explore different perspectives to examine globalization from a global viewpoint. True to its global character, the *Theory for a Global Age* series will be available for online access worldwide via Creative Commons licensing, aiming to stimulate wide debate within academia and beyond.

Previously published by Bloomsbury:
Connected Sociologies
Gurminder K. Bhambra

Eurafrica: The Untold History of European Integration and Colonialism
Peo Hansen and Stefan Jonsson

On Sovereignty and Other Political Delusions
Joan Cocks

Postcolonial Piracy: Media Distribution and Cultural Production in the Global South
Edited by Lars Eckstein and Anja Schwarz

The Black Pacific: Anticolonial Struggles and Oceanic Connections
Robbie Shilliam

Democracy and Revolutionary Politics
Neera Chandhoke

Published by Manchester University Press:
Debt as Power
Richard H. Robbins and Tim Di Muzio

John Dewey

The Global Public and Its Problems

John Narayan

Manchester University Press

Copyright © John Narayan 2016

The right of John Narayan to be identified as the author of this work has been asserted by him in accordance with the Copyright, Designs and Patents Act 1988.

Published by Manchester University Press
Altrincham Street, Manchester M1 7JA

www.manchesteruniversitypress.co.uk

This work is published subject to a Creative Commons Attribution Non-commercial No Derivatives Licence. You may share this work for non-commercial purposes only, provided you give attribution to the copyright holder and the publisher. For permission to publish commercial versions please contact Manchester University Press.

British Library Cataloguing-in-Publication Data
A catalogue record for this book is available from the British Library

ISBN 978 1 7849 93245   hardback
      978 1 5261 41873   paperback
      978 1 5261 01020   open access

First published 2016

This edition first published 2019

The publisher has no responsibility for the persistence or accuracy of URLs for any external or third-party internet websites referred to in this book, and does not guarantee that any content on such websites is, or will remain, accurate or appropriate.

Typeset by
Integra Software Services Pvt. Ltd.

For Rosie

Contents

Series Editor's Foreword	ix
Acknowledgements	x
Introduction: Retrieving a 'Global' American Philosopher	1
The enigma of democratic globalization	4
Back to the future	9
Outline of the book	10
A ventriloquist's disclaimer	13
1 Creative Democracy	15
Unfashionable democracy	15
Problematic states and their problematic publics:	
The futility of state theory	19
The history of publics and the spectre of violence	28
Making the case for democracy as a way of life	31
Democracy as a way of life + political democracy =	
creative democracy	36
2 The Global Democrat	41
The Great Society as the First Great Globalization	42
Dewey's plea for a global Great Community	45
Global creative democracy	51
3 The Obstacles to Creative Democracy at Home and Abroad	55
The eclipse of the public	57
The national and global eclipse of creative democracy	66
4 Social Intelligence and Equality	75
The habits of social intelligence	77
The planning society	85

Democracy and equality	88
Global democracy and equality	95

5   New Lessons from the Old Professor   103
   Lesson 1: A Great Society does not equal
   a Great Community   104
   Lesson 2: The Great Community and the nation   106
   Lesson 3: Democracy begins at home   109
   Lesson 4: The spectre of bourgeois democracy
   must be exorcised!   115
   Global democracy: A new name for an old problem   119

Conclusion: Inheriting the Task of Creative Democracy   127

Notes   131
Bibliography   155
Index   165

Series Editor's Foreword

The fate of democracy under conditions of neoliberal globalization is the focus for John Narayan's comprehensive re-examination of the work of philosopher and proto-sociologist, John Dewey. While, as Narayan argues, Dewey did not himself make a sustained argument for global democracy, a powerful idea of global democracy can be constructed from his philosophical and sociological writings. In this way, in *John Dewey: The Global Public and Its Problems*, Narayan expertly demonstrates the continuing relevance of John Dewey's thought for the consideration of contemporary problems of modern sovereignty and questions of political and democratic legitimacy in a global age.

Narayan starts with a discussion of Dewey's understanding of democracy as a creative process of reform and renewal. This discussion is located in terms of examining the global conditions of 'the Great Society' and the global institutions and publics that are part of its functioning at the larger scale. While the focus is strongly on 'the global', there is also consideration of the national contexts which dominate in the debates and political practices of democracy. As Narayan sets out, democracy, for Dewey, had to be articulated both 'at home' and 'abroad'. In the latter sections of the book, Narayan pays due attention to the ideas of global justice and equality that are often neglected aspects of Dewey's thought and makes a robust argument for egalitarian democracy on a global scale.

The book is an excellent illustration of one of the motivating aspects of the Theory for a Global Age series, namely, a concern to reconsider existing understandings of the global such that we might better understand our contemporary global condition. Dewey's call to renew and refresh our thinking in light of changes is nicely exemplified by Narayan's own rethinking of Dewey's thought for our contemporary times.

Gurminder K. Bhambra

Acknowledgements

Although the intellectual process is often a lonely existence, it is undoubtedly not a sole endeavour. Indeed, without the help of others it would be nigh on impossible. I wish to thank the following for their help during the formation of this piece.

To my wonderful wife, Rosie Narayan, whose intellect and unconditional love and support have always been a place where I could take refuge or draw strength from whenever the books have started to hit back! This would not have been possible without you.

I must also mention the life form who I spend the majority of my time with during the day, our family dog, Nina, who has spent most days sleeping in her basket under my desk as I edited the manuscript, and whose daily walks have provided the thinking space needed to get over any bump in the road along the way.

I would also like to extend my deepest gratitude to:

The Economic and Social Research Council for funding the study upon which this work is based and the University of Nottingham for providing the institutional support to complete the research.

Professor John Holmwood for his intellectual companionship and general tolerance of my unabashed trait of disagreeing with him. Thank you for the support through the years and the hard work that you have put into my own work.

Professor Gurminder K. Bhambra whose support for this project is only outweighed by the support she has given to my most recent intellectual endeavours. Thank you for helping me wade through the murky waters of academia!

My wonderful friends: Ross and Sian Abbinnett, Kehinde and Nicole Andrews, Martin Culliney, Ruairi Hughes, Uzo and Heidi Ibechukwu and Christopher and Louise Twardowski. It is a privilege to count on you as friends. I love you all!

I must also send love to the little ones: Simon Abbinnett, Assata and Kadiri Andrews, Esme Ibechukwu, Naeva Twardowski, my little cousin, Eleanor Wood, and my nephew, Gustav, and niece, Galia Nickson. You all promise hope to a desperate world.

A special thank you must be sent to the Narayan clan for their support of my intellectual endeavours down the years. Also to the Browns and Nicksons, especially Lorna and Joe, for welcoming me into their family. And I must mention the Dass family in Fiji, whose reconnection has brought extra happiness to the writing process.

A special thanks must also be reserved for Rosie's mum, Louise Brown, and Tilly the dog. A lot of this work was initially conceived at Louise's house during my PhD and she even took to correcting the manuscript's many spelling mistakes. Thank you for your support over the years.

Finally, I would like to thank my mother, Evelyn Narayan, and my father, Vijendra Narayan, for their love and for dreaming for me long before I knew what it was to dream. I owe you everything.

Introduction: Retrieving a 'Global' American Philosopher

There are two requests I should like to make to readers of the volume, not to forestall criticism but that it may be rendered, perhaps, more pertinent. Three lectures do not permit one to say all he thinks, nor even all that he believes that he knows. Omission of topics and themes does not, accordingly, signify that I should have passed them by in a more extended treatment. I particularly regret the enforced omission of reference to the relation of liberalism to international affairs. I should also like to remind readers that not everything can be said in the same breath and that it is necessary to stress first one aspect and then another of the general subject. So I hope that what is said will be taken as a whole and also in comparison and contrast with alternative methods of social action. (LW11: 4)[1]

It might seem rather bizarre to claim that a return to the work of John Dewey can offer a greater appreciation of globalization and global democracy at the start of the twenty-first century. Dewey appears to be a creature of a wholly different epoch; born in 1859, the year Darwin published *Origin of the Species* and just short of eighteen months before the Battle of Fort Sumter, Dewey's life would end only some six years after the beginning of the 'Cold War'. To read his body of work is therefore to enter a world that does not include bearing witness to some of the most momentous events of American and world history in the twentieth century. This includes the success of the American Civil Rights Movement, the Vietnam War and the winds of change that flattened European imperialism and empire. This is to say nothing of events such as the rise and fall of the Bretton Woods regime, the hegemonic ascent of neo-liberalism, the end of the Cold War and the rise of communications technology such as the Internet. Dewey's world thus appears to be alien to contemporary concerns about rampant globalization and the need to move democracy beyond the confines of the nation state to regulate a runaway world.

Indeed, one might also label the attempt to call Dewey a 'global' thinker pure and utter philosophical folly in the first place. After all, there doesn't seem to be, philosophically at least, anything more quintessentially American than Dewey and his brand of philosophical pragmatism. This view is common amongst various critical interpreters of Dewey's work, who saw pragmatism as a foil for American capitalism (Westbrook 2005: 139–41). Famously, Bertrand Russell (1909) labelled the work of Dewey and his fellow philosophical pragmatists, such as William James and Charles Sanders Pierce, as little more than the philosophical accomplice to American corporate capitalism. This viewpoint was repeated by Lewis Mumford (1926: 77) in the 1920s, who charged Dewey and his fellow pragmatists with a form of philosophical 'acquiescence', which propounded an uncritical body of philosophy that was 'permeated by the smell of the Gilded Age'. Whilst Martin Heidegger (1977: 153) would label philosophical pragmatism as the 'American interpretation of Americanism', a philosophy that simply replicated American capitalism's 'technological frenzy' and constant 'reorganization of man'.

In the light of these statements, an uninformed reader would seemingly be quite justified in believing Dewey to be a 'local' American philosopher, whose work is unable to offer us in the present any insight about 'global' issues. On one hand, one cannot deny that Dewey was a local philosopher whose accent was unmistakably American. In writing back to Mumford, for instance, Dewey argued that pragmatism was not the expression of American industrialism but rather the re-articulation of American values that were now opposed to those 'most in evidence' in the Gilded Age (LW3: 127). These were the values of a 'radical democratic tradition' that could be traced back to the history of the United States of America and the words and creeds of Lincoln, Jefferson and Emerson (Bernstein 2010: 88). From these democratic foundations, Dewey came to a profound understanding that democracy was fragile and needed to be rejuvenated and reinterpreted to live up to its ideal of a 'democratic way of life'. Dewey's philosophical oeuvre, and in particular his political philosophy in works such as *The Public and Its Problems* (LW2) and *Liberalism and Social Action* (LW11), therefore often looked to pit 'America against itself' so that the country could achieve the democratic hopes and dreams that were the foundation of its independence (Westbrook 2005: 140). In this vein, Dewey's philosophy can be seen as an earlier incarnation of the democratic spirit that Richard Rorty (1999) evoked when he sought to show how intellectual labour could help American citizens to 'achieve our country'.

On the other hand, however, Dewey was not just concerned with American democracy but rather American democracy in a global context. From the conquest and founding of the North American continent by the Europeans, or the importation of chattel slaves from Africa, to its war of independence right through to the nascent industrial world Dewey would be born into, America had always been a country animated and related to global flows of people, technology and politics. The American Civil War (1861–65) in which Dewey grew up in was fought just as much as a result of the diametrically opposed views on international trade policy between Southern and Northern states as it was fought over the immorality of chattel slavery. At the end of his life, Dewey would see the global ramifications of the atomic bomb and the emergence of the Truman Doctrine that effectively committed the United States to a global struggle against the Soviet Union and her allies. In between Dewey visited or taught in Europe, China, Turkey, Mexico, the USSR, and aged seventy-eight, he departed in 1937 for Mexico to chair an international committee created to inquire into the charges made by the Soviet state against Leon Trotsky (Cochran 2010: 310). When one adds to this that Dewey lived through the Spanish-American War, the First World War, the rise of communism and fascism, the Great Depression and (the *fait accompli* that was) the Second World War, it is clear that Dewey was an American inhabitant of a global world.

Whilst Dewey's political philosophy was thus a creature of late nineteenth century and early twentieth-century America, it was more importantly about America in a globalized and interdependent world, or rather what Dewey called 'The Great Society'. Indeed, as the preface to *Liberalism and Social Action* cited earlier makes clear, even when Dewey could not find the room to talk about the global context in his philosophy it was never too far from his mind. This dual aspect of Dewey's life and his work, where he was an American living in a global world, appears to have been lost in translation throughout the years. This book aims to show how the retrieval of the 'global' John Dewey not only highlights that it was the global context of American democracy that forced Dewey's political philosophy into the task of 'restoring the spirit of America and its origin and propelling it, revised and renewed, into the future' (Martin 2002: 397–8). But that the global context also led Dewey to become a fully fledged global democrat, who sought to revise and renew American democracy along and within global dimensions. The overall aim of this book is to show how the fruits of Dewey's attempts to reconstruct democracy, both at home and abroad, in the first half of the twentieth century provide rich food for thought about our twenty-first-century attempts to rethink democracy in the age of globalization.[2]

The enigma of democratic globalization

The obvious question that arises out of the claim that we need to recover a 'global' Dewey is why do we need such retrieval in the first place? The answer revolves around the relationship between globalization and democracy. The fate of democracy in the age of globalization, especially globalization under the auspices of neo-liberalism, has preoccupied scholars across the social sciences since the fall of the Berlin Wall (Fine 2007; Calhoun 2008). This preoccupation has revolved around the argument that globalization demands that we become post-Westphalian in 'a deep ontological sense' and let go 'not only of the idea of the sovereign state, but also of the individualistic basis for the establishment of sovereign authority formalised by Thomas Hobbes at the same time as the Treaty of Westphalia...' (Dryzek 2012: 113–14). Within this narrative, globalization is not to be taken, as it so often is, as a word to be causally thrown around or as some sort of theoretical cushion that appears to mould to the posterior of whoever sits upon it. Rather, propelled by neo-liberal imperatives, modern globalization is said to have unleashed a historically unprecedented form of interconnectedness through intercontinental or interregional forms of trade, production and finance that have fundamentally altered the status of the nation state and national democracy (Held 2010: 28–9).[3]

The primary effect of neo-liberal globalization is that 'modern sovereignty', where autonomous nation states exercise unquestionable authority within bounded political communities and resolve their differences with one another through reason of state and diplomacy, is said to have collapsed (Held and McGrew 2007: 211). This is because neo-liberal globalization has encouraged the deterritorialization of political authority and sovereignty away from the nation state and the subsequent reterritorialization of such power beyond the nation state. This now not only makes the nation state largely subservient to the tenets of free-market economics but also establishes the authority of global governance institutions (IMF, WTO, World Bank) and global markets over the nation state (Hardt and Negri 1999; Habermas 2001).

The ramifications of neo-liberal globalization and the supposed collapse of modern sovereignty for the legitimacy and power of national democracy are stark. If we take democracy to be the sign of a legitimate order and define its normative meaning as all affected persons being included, either directly or through their representatives, in the deliberation and formation of decisions and legislation which shape their common circumstance and destinies, then it becomes clear that globalization's creation of global interconnectedness and the decline of modern sovereignty render nation states incapable of securing democratic accountability for their citizens. The embrace of a post-Westphalian ontology and very normative strictures of democracy therefore demands the extension of '...political decision making capabilities beyond national borders...' (Habermas 2012: 15) at the same time as the scope of decisions within them is also being undercut.

Those who embrace such a post-Westphalian ontology include a variety of scholars who are not necessarily happy bedfellows. However, they are united by the belief that statist solutions, where global democracy is envisaged to centre on multilateral collaboration between democratic nation states, are unable to achieve global democracy. This includes modern statist positions, which argue that democracy beyond the state is secure when democracy within the state is secure. Whilst post-Westphalian ideas of global democracy see the state and its democracy as having provided key pivots for global democracy, such as forming the UN system, their belief is that such a system is still a deficient and flawed medium to achieve global democracy in present circumstances. This centres on the internal political and economic stratification within states, the transnational nature of global interconnectedness, the inability of national leaders to further global democracy beyond national interests and the continuing hegemony of rich and powerful nations at the international level. Whilst the state should play a part in global democracy, post-Westphalian positions believe that global democracy cannot begin and end with the state and interstate relations (Scholte 2012: 4–6).

Following Cochran (2002), we can divide these post-Westphalian positions on global democracy very roughly into those who favour 'top-down' pathways to global democracy and those who favour 'bottom-up' pathways. Top-down pathways can be seen as revolving around the idea of modern cosmopolitanism. Premised upon the theoretical foundations provided by Kant and the work of twentieth-century world federalists, modern cosmopolitanism purports that the world should be taken as a unit of society that has political rights and obligations transcending its nation state-based counterparts (Brown and Held 2010). This has seen a plethora of work arguing for the supplementing and transcending of elements of liberal democracy's national framework to regional and/or global dimensions (Held 1995,

2004; Habermas, 2006; Archibugi 2008; Hale et al., 2013). This would see nation states pool sovereignty through submitting their national interests to regional (EU) and global governance (UN) institutions, and the extending of liberal democracy's national framework of citizenship rights, civil society (Kaldor 2003), the public sphere (Bohman 2007) and elements of political democracy, such as parliaments and political parties (Patomäki 2011), from national to regional or global levels.

Modern cosmopolitanism has come under criticism for privileging the roles of elites and a form of spatial globalism that revolves around global institutions and organizations without examining how global democracy is linked to local, national and regional democracy (Smith and Brassett 2008; Calhoun 2010). At the same time, modern cosmopolitanism is also accused of a failure to tackle the global economic inequalities that are created and perpetuated by neo-liberal globalization (Hardt and Negri 2004) and of universalizing Eurocentric ideas of citizenship, sovereignty, human rights and democracy without any transcultural dialogue with non-Western epistemologies (Rao 2010; Bhambra 2011; Hobson 2012).

To circumvent the failings of modern cosmopolitanism, a wide range of authors have attempted to reimagine global democracy from below and have argued for bottom-up strategies for achieving global democracy. These include conceiving spaces such as global civil society (Brassett and Smith 2010), the international public sphere (Dryzek 2006, 2010) and the World Social Forum (Sen and Escobar 2007) as arenas that retain their independence from governance institutions and provide a platform for social movements, activists and citizens to communicate and politically organize on a global level. More radical positions look to social movements such as the Zapatistas, anti-globalization and Occupy Movement not only to transcend the spatial globalism and Eurocentrism of modern cosmopolitanism but also to displace global capitalist relations in the formation of a new and novel form of global democracy (Hardt and Negri 1999, 2004, 2011).

Post-Westphalian global democracy is not without its own critics, however. As Scholte (2012: 10) points out, some see global democracy as an 'oxymoron' because democracy beyond the space of the local or national container becomes impossible to manage or implement (Dhal 1999, 2001). This has led to the argument that the way to secure greater global democracy is to actually 'deglobalize' the global economy and allow nations to assert their sovereignty in economic and political matters (Bello 2005, 2013). The debate surrounding post-Westphalian ideas of global democracy can therefore be seen as a site of competing and unresolved dualisms. On one hand, there is a dualism between statist and post-Westphalian ideas of global democracy. On the other hand, within ideas of post-Westphalian democracy there is also a dualism between top-down and bottom-up approaches to global democracy.

These unresolved dualisms, which plague ideas of global democracy, are not mere theoretical abstractions. Behind them resides a current world order governed by neo-liberal globalization and insufficient democratic control. Neo-liberal imperatives, which identify private markets and free economic enterprise as meeting human needs and freedom vis-à-vis largely inefficient state intervention and regulation, have increased systemic inequality within and between states and regions of the world. Moreover, forms of global governance are both undemocratic and unable to govern globalization democratically (Chang 2007; Wade 2009a, 2009b; Rodrik 2011). The result of failing to increase democratic control over neo-liberal globalization could not be bleaker. At the dawn of the twenty-first century, there are very few theoretical debates that have such potential practical permutations and relevancy than the theoretical debate about the best way to secure global democracy. Indeed, the debate about global democracy would appear to centre on nothing short of the survival or extinction of the human race:

> Unresolved global challenges such as nuclear proliferation, global inequality, global infectious diseases, environmental degradation, and financial crises not only risk affecting the life chances of men, women, and children across the world in the future, but do so now in numerous ways. At the core of daily human insecurity, as well as uncertainty

created by risks ranging from new forms of terrorism to nuclear war or accelerating climate change, lie fundamental issues of survival, freedom, the rule of law, and social justice. (Hale et al. 2013: 311)

Back to the future

It might seem counter-intuitive to attempt to interpret how we can democratize neo-liberal globalization through the work of a philosopher who died midway through the twentieth century. However, through returning to and recovering the neglected global dimensions of John Dewey's political philosophy and international writings, this book will aim to highlight the 'global' Dewey. I argue that his insights about globalization and democracy can contribute towards present theoretical debates about globalization and global democracy. Moreover, John Dewey's work from the end of the First World War onwards prefigures an approach to global democracy that not only dispels the dualisms that plague modern ideas of global democracy but also has important points to make about the role of national democracy in the expansion of democracy beyond the confines of the nation state.

The book discloses the 'global Dewey' through examining how his works – especially *The Public and Its Problems* (LW2) – set out an evolutionary form of global and national democracy in response to a rapidly globalizing economy. The global dimensions of Dewey's thought have received relatively little study and although they are underappreciated they provide valuable lessons for those of us in the twenty-first century who hold out hopes for global democracy. These lessons centre on how Dewey's work illuminates the following:

- The problem of globalization and democracy is rooted in the emergence of the First Great Globalization of the nineteenth century.
- The rise of globalization and increased industrial complexity does not necessarily create reflexive and cosmopolitan individuals.

- Nationalism and national democracy are not the archenemies of planetary democracy.
- The fate of extending democracy beyond the nation state is twined with the fate of democracy at the national level, and the nation state is the starting point for any form of planetary democracy.
- Liberal capitalism and democracy are, to a large extent, incompatible with one another.

Above all, the book will conclude that Deweyan lessons highlight that what we often take to be the problems of 'globalization', the collapse of 'modern sovereignty' and 'global democracy' are simply new ways of expressing old concerns and debates. Those of us in the present would therefore be well served by returning to Dewey's reflections on these old concerns as a source of new insights into our own present of globalization and its deadly discontents.

Outline of the book

The book consists of five chapters. Chapters 1 and 2 highlight how Dewey's defence of democracy in the context of what he denotes as the Great Society leads him to confront the problems of globalization and global democracy. Chapter 1 thus returns to Dewey's 1927 text *The Public and Its Problems* and fleshes out how his conception of 'creative democracy' defines democracy as an evolutionary ideal whose institutions change and adapt to the demands of the environment. This entails re-examining Dewey's debate with Walter Lippmann and democratic realism about the nature of the state, publics, expertise and the value of democracy and outlining his subsequent argument that publics, government and consequently the state are historically relative properties. This is followed by an examination of Dewey's argument that democracy is the best way to deal with such historical relativity due its ability to efficiently update the institutions of government without unnecessary recourse to violent revolution or the suppression of others. The chapter ends by outlining how Dewey believed the ideal of 'creative democracy' conjoined the ideal of democracy (what he called 'democracy as a way of life') with a practical agenda of reforming and renewing what he saw as the institutions and practices of 'political democracy'.

Chapter 2 explores how Dewey's conception of creative democracy had global connotations. This entails recovering how Dewey's political philosophy of publics and democracy was forged with globalization and the extension of democracy beyond the nation state in mind. This is achieved by firstly contextualizing Dewey's work from the 1920s onwards and its evocation of the emergence of 'The Great Society' as being a reaction to the First Great Globalization, which had taken place in the nineteenth century and continued through the early parts of the twentieth century. The chapter continues by examining how Dewey's texts from *The Public and Its Problems* onwards called for the creation of a global Great Community and global democracy to regulate the global dimensions of the Great Society. The chapter concludes by highlighting how Dewey believed that global democracy was a realizable endeavour and outlines some of his recommendations for how it should be practised through the empowerment of publics and global institutions.

Chapter 3 will examine how Dewey problematized his own conception of democracy through arguing that the public within modern nation states was 'eclipsed' under the regime he called 'bourgeois democracy'. In this scenario, citizen publics were unable to map the forces affecting their lives and disenchanted with a political democracy that had been captured by the interests of capital. It has become the norm to read Dewey's account of the eclipse of the public and the stunting of creative democracy as simply being concerned with the American nation state. However, the chapter will conclude by demonstrating that Dewey's claim that the Great Society had no 'political agencies worthy of it' extended to matters of global democracy and that he twined the fate of democracy beyond the nation state to democracy within the nation state.

Chapter 4 shifts the terrain of Dewey's global focus to ideas of global justice and equality. This chapter demonstrates that Dewey's idea of global democracy was linked with an idea of global equality, which would secure social intelligence on a global scale. The logical result of this argument is a radical conception of global justice and the need for economic equality within and beyond nations. This revolves around examining how Dewey's idea of creative democracy was based upon a form of deliberation he called social intelligence and how social intelligence is essentially an adoption of the 'scientific attitude of the mind' into moral and political matters. It will be argued that Dewey did not believe that liberal capitalism's culture and political economy could support the conditions of equality, which would make creative democracy through social intelligence possible. Dewey's politics of democratic socialism subsequently reveals his views on the relationship between economic and political equality within the Great Society. The final section highlights how Dewey's views on economic and political equality translate into an argument for the extension of a global egalitarianism, which would allow all nations of the world to pursue the democratic way of life.

To conclude the study, Chapter 5 turns to outlining what I believe are the four main lessons Dewey provides about global democracy. All four of these lessons foresee the contemporary obstacles faced in moving democracy beyond the nation state and, importantly, how Dewey realized that democracy abroad was impossible without democracy at home. Moreover, these lessons revolve around what we can denote as Dewey's rooted cosmopolitanism, which argues that without a thriving democracy within the nation state there can be very little chance of democracy beyond the nation state. The chapter concludes by arguing that Dewey's work on the problems of bourgeois democracy at home and abroad highlights significant gaps in post-Westphalian conceptions of global democracy. This will reveal that the nature, political efficacy or viability, of any conception of 'global democracy' in the twenty-first century can only be adequately conceptualized by revisiting and confronting Deweyan concerns about the political efficacy or viability of publics and their relation to democratic praxis within the nation state.

A ventriloquist's disclaimer

Before I start my exposition of John Dewey as a global philosopher, a quick note about intellectual interpretation must be made. Robert Westbrook (2005: 177), perhaps John Dewey's key intellectual biographer, makes a pertinent point about intellectual history when he states that intellectual historians bear a responsibility to read philosophers accurately in order to illuminate how these figures can provide useful guidance on our present problems. In the act of ventriloquism that is intellectual history we therefore bear the responsibility of making our philosophical puppet utter words it would have uttered if he or she were actually alive or present in the room. This is less about a rigid conception of objective truth, argues Westbrook, but rather a rough and ready rule to stop us imagining intellectual playmates who may never have existed in the first place.[4] In this book, I try to follow Westbrook's advice as much as I can, but I do bend Westbrook's rule for intellectual historians slightly, not by elucidating an argument Dewey would never have made, but by outlining an argument Dewey did not outline in one systematic statement but one he could have made in a systematic way if had chosen to. Dewey did not make a great systematic statement on global democracy but a philosophy of global democracy is scattered throughout his body of work. Indeed, Dewey's lack of a book on global democracy seems more due to a lack of time and the fact that he was busy writing as a concerned American citizen in a global world. However, as we shall see, this makes perfect sense when you understand Dewey's belief in the fact that democracy at home was fundamentally linked to democracy abroad.

1

Creative Democracy

Optimism about democracy is today under a cloud. (LW2: 304)

Unfashionable democracy

When Dewey published *The Public and Its Problems* in 1927, democracy had become somewhat of an unfashionable aspiration, with populations in Europe beginning to turn to the extreme Left and Right for their political settlements. In Russia the October Revolution was nearly ten years old, in Italy Mussolini had been in power for three years and in Germany both volumes of *Mein Kampf* had been published. At home in the United States of America, even the pretence of democracy in the country had come under attack.[1] The catalyst for this attack on American democracy revolved around the dissipation of post–First World War optimism about reconstructing America in fairer and more just terms. Whilst Progressives put forward ideas for economic justice and fairness, such reforms were 'strangled' by older patterns of thought and behaviour that re-emerged in the climate of revolution (Kloppenberg 1986). The breakdown of this optimism amongst American progressives in turn gave way to the rise of trenchant intellectual critiques of the suitability of democratic government for 1920s America. Conducted by American political scientists and commentators, these critiques of the suitability of democratic government would form what became known as 'democratic realism'. And by the 1930s, the paradigm had become near hegemonic in American social science (Westbrook 1991: 281–6).

The main charge of democratic realism was that democracy was now unable to provide a stable or efficient government for advanced industrial societies. For democratic realism, the institutions of democratic government, which were based on democracy's core beliefs in the capacity of all people for rational political action and the belief in maximizing civic participation in public life, were in fact counterproductive to good government in industrial societies (Westbrook 1991: 281–2). The main articulation of this position was to be found in the work of Walter Lippmann and his two treatises against standard liberal thought, *Public Opinion* (1922) and *The Phantom Public* (1925). Within these works, Lippmann puts forward the idea that America had entered into the Great Society, which made the core beliefs of democracy unrealizable.

The concept of the Great Society, adapted by both Lippmann and later Dewey from Graham Wallas' (1914) book of the same name, was essentially shorthand for the complex industrial and mass consumer society America had become in the aftermath of the First World War. The end of the American Civil War had signalled that America would use its vast reserves of raw materials and land to become a continental nation state with an industrial economy rather than being a decentralized federation of states with a slave-based agrarian economy.[2] This process had seen America not only master the steam-, coal- and railway-based technologies and industries of the first industrial revolution, but also become the leader of the second industrial revolution of the late nineteenth and early twentieth centuries. This saw the systematic application of science to the industrial process in the new oil-, electricity- and chemical-based industries of automobiles, synthetic material production and consumer durables (Frieden 2006: 152; Morris 2011: 510; Lind 2012: 5–10). The result was that, as early as 1914, the US economy, in both absolute figures and per capita terms, had overtaken Britain as the biggest economy in the world. By 1919, due in part to the economic consequences of the First World War, US economic output was greater than all of Europe (Kennedy 1987: 242–4).

Dewey argued that the Great Society's improvements in industrial production, travel and transportation (railways, cars), media (radio, newspapers) and communications (telegraph, telephone) not only eliminated distance as an economic and social factor but also created 'interaction and interdependence' on an unprecedented complex and wide scale (LW2: 307). In industry, for example, the new corporations of 1920s America such as General Motors, Ford and General Electric did not just produce oligopolistic industries but had become vertically integrated entities. Such vertically integrated corporations and the widespread use of electricity, cheaper steel production, the chemical industry and the advent of the assembly line thus delivered mass industrial production.[3]

The move from an agrarian to such an advanced capitalist society had essentially brought about massive changes in the day-to-day life of Americans. The revolution in corporate structure and industrial production, which saw consumer durables such as cars, radios and refrigerators become the driving force of economic growth, had seen a concomitant revolution of mass consumption. And as productivity soared, the prices of consumer durables dropped. Ford's Model T, for example, reduced in price from $700 (US) in 1910 to $350 (US) in 1916 and by 1916 it took only six months for the average American to earn enough money to buy one. By 1929, Americans were driving some 26 million cars or trucks. And this is to say nothing of the 20 million phones installed by 1930, new public highways and railway lines, the advent of chain stores and modern advertising, radio set sales, electric stoves and heaters, consumer credit and the fact that by 1924 one could even buy sliced bread (Leuchtenburg 1993: 178–202; Frieden 2006: 62–3, 155–72).

For writers such as Lippmann, the emergence of the Great Society created a far too complex industrial and corporate environment for a normal citizen to exercise rational political judgement about how such a society should be governed. For Lippmann the common citizen was being driven along by industrial innovation and expertise that they could not grasp and was also distracted by mass consumption. As a result, modern citizens were incapable of grasping their immediate present, their own interests and essentially living in a world they 'cannot see, [do] not understand and [are] unable to direct' (Lippmann 1925: 4). The democratic goal of maximizing the civic participation of all citizens in public life was thus simply 'bad only in the sense that it is bad for a fat man to try to be a ballet dancer' (Lippmann 1925: 29). The only solution, argued Lippmann, was for normal citizens to give up the concept of self-rule and move towards a system of elitism, whereby experts who are in a position to grasp the complexities of the Great Society would create and enact social policy. In this context, citizens would only play the role of siding with or against different elites, playing no role in policy formation and simply voting for the 'Ins when things are going well and the Outs when things are going badly' (Lippmann 1925: 126).

In Dewey's eyes, the attacks upon democracy by communism, fascism and democratic realism were bound to fail miserably or end up in violence and bloodshed. Quite simply, democratic realism's quasi-Platonism and communism and fascism's authoritarianism, which held experts or rulers as the only ones capable to enact policies that would be wise and beneficial to the common good of society, contradicted the historical record. The emergence and practice of democracy itself had shown that it is only through wide consultation and discussion that wider social needs and common goods are uncovered. As Dewey colourfully put it, the man '... who wears the shoe knows best that it pinches and where it pinches, even if the expert shoe maker is the best judge of how the trouble is to be remedied' (LW2: 364). To subsequently remove the input of the masses and leave government policy to an elite was to create a class closed off from the knowledge of the needs that they were supposed to serve. Dewey therefore feared that rule by an elite group in which the masses could not express their needs would resemble an oligarchy managed in the interests of the few rather than the many. And as Dewey reminded his readers, such fears were not mere abstractions when history patently highlighted how the '... world has suffered more from leaders and authorities than from the so-called folly of masses' (LW2: 365).[4]

The Public and Its Problems is thus best seen as attempting to walk along the path that Dewey believed the far Left and Right in Europe and democratic realism in America shed light upon but refused to travel: the contemporary problem of democracy within the Great Society. Moreover, Dewey sets himself the goal of answering the question that he believed Lippmann and others hastily skimmed over by rendering the masses innately incapable of civic organization: Why is the contemporary public seemingly unable to intelligently perform the tasks that democracy requires of them? To accomplish this, Dewey embarks upon two interrelated tasks within *The Public and Its Problems*. The first task, which I examine below, involves Dewey reconstructing the concept of democracy as a form of 'creative democracy', simultaneously redefining the political concepts of the 'state', 'public', 'government' and ultimately 'democracy' itself. As I outline in Chapter 2, this task saw Dewey stretch those concepts beyond the remit of the nation state. The second task, which we will discuss in Chapter 3, involves the examination of why the democracy of Dewey's present within the Great Society bore a poor resemblance to his own vision of democracy as a way of life.[5]

Problematic states and their problematic publics: The futility of state theory

It was Dewey's belief that the meaning of democracy and the justification for its practice had seemingly become lost in the hubris of democratic realism. In the journey to reconstruct and redefine the concept of democracy, Dewey initially returns to another, if not the most, perennial question of political philosophy: What is the origin and nature of the state? In reference to what he believed were prior flawed theories of the state, from the works of Aristotle through to and beyond Hegel, Dewey cautions his readers that the 'moment we utter the words "The State" a score of intellectual ghosts rise to obscure our vision' (LW2: 240).

This obfuscation, Dewey contended, arose because theories of the state resorted to mythological 'state-forming forces' or 'political instincts' to explain the state and its functions. For example, Aristotle's claim that man by nature is an animal that lives in a state and Social Contract Theory's claim that the state emerges after a fictional state of nature tell us nothing about how actual states come into being or why states take on different forms at different points in history. Such theories merely repackaged the outcome of a given social process (Greek City State/Liberal Democracy) as its cause and reduplicated it in '... a so called causal force the effects to be accounted for.' Ultimately, Dewey charged, that such theories hold no more explanatory value than the statement that opium had sleep-inducing effects because of its 'dormative powers' (LW2: 240–1).

Following his dismissal of the explanatory value of prior theories of the state, Dewey begins his own analysis of politics – its institutional forms and practices – from the very empirical starting point he believes the aforementioned theories neglect: the history of human activity and its consequences (LW2: 243). Building upon his prior engagement with Darwin's theory of evolution and the psychology of William James, Dewey puts forward an argument for the social nature of both the self and morality. The foundation of this argument is that like all objects within nature, human beings exist in an environment where 'conjoint, combined, associated action is a universal trait of the behaviour of things' (LW2: 257). What we take to be human nature or what we take to be the human 'self' is said by Dewey not to be an immutable property or instinct which individuals then utilize to interact with their environment, but rather an entity which is produced as the outcome of the interaction of the human organism with its environment.[6]

This interaction of the human organism with its environment takes place through what Dewey denotes as *habits*, which 'bind us to orderly and established ways of action' (LW2: 335).[7] In this sense, habits are not simply recurrent or routine ways of behaving but rather acquired predispositions or modes of response, which generate ease, skill and interest when individuals interact with their environment:

> For we are given to thinking of a habit as simply a recurrent external mode of action, like smoking or swearing, being neat or negligent

in clothes and person, taking exercise or playing games. But habit reaches even more significantly down into the very structure of the self; it signifies a building up of and solidifying of certain desires; an increased sensitiveness and responsiveness to certain stimuli, a confirmed or impaired capacity to attend to and think about certain things. Habit covers in other words the very make up of desire, intent, choice, disposition which gives an act its voluntary quality. (LW7: 170-1)

The important point to consider here, however, is that we do not simply create our habits out of thin air, but rather acquire and learn our habits from what Dewey calls 'social customs'. Much like the language we speak, individuals inherit and form their personal moral habits from the uniformities, habits or set ways of conduct of the respective social groups they are born into or are associated with throughout their lives. From birth onwards individuals find that established social customs, which saturate such habits with meaning, are taught and transmitted to them through the associated life they have with other humans (MW14: 43–52). As Dewey points out, the sailor, miner, fisherman and farmer think about their actions, but their thoughts fall within the framework of accustomed occupations and social relations. What an individual actually is as a self – that is, how an individual thinks and acts – is ultimately dependent upon the nature and movement of their associated life (LW5: 275).

These habits and customs are structured through what Dewey calls a society's 'cultural matrix'.[8] The idea of a 'cultural matrix' thus corresponds to a society's socio-economic, technological and intellectual (religion/science/philosophy/politics) practices, which determine the associative relations (occupations, family structures and geographical links) and the meanings (habits/customs) attached to those associated relations by various social groups (LW12: 481-2). As such, a society's cultural matrix provides an:

> ...inalienable and ineradicable framework of conceptions which is not of our own making, but given to us ready-made by society – a whole apparatus of concepts and categories, within which and by

which individual thinking, however daring and original, is compelled to move. (LW12: 482)

It may be tempting to think from the above that Dewey assigns priority of society over the individual and that the individual is only an expression of society. However, Dewey's point is that the human self is produced through pre-existent associations and the social customs of other humans not society at large (M14: 44, cf. Gouinlock 1972: 105–6). This does not discount that social customs can stretch across society but such a subtle distinction highlights how societies are not uniform but rather pluralistic entities:

> Society is one word, but many things. Men associate together in all kinds of ways and for all kinds of purposes. One man is concerned in a multitude of diverse groups, in which his associates may be quite different. It often seems as if they had nothing in common except that they are modes of associated life. Within every larger social organisation there are numerous minor groups; not only political subdivisions but industrial, scientific, religious, associations. There are political parties with differing aims, social sets, cliques, gangs, corporations, partnerships, groups bound closely together by ties of blood, and so in endless variety. In many modern states, and in some ancient, there is great diversity of populations, of varying languages, religions, moral codes and traditions. From this standpoint, many a modern political unit, one of large cities for example, is a congeries of loosely associated societies rather than an inclusive and permeating community of action and thought. (MW9: 87–8)

At any given synchronic moment within a cultural matrix, there exist individuals and groups who share different associated relations and different habits and different social customs. Indeed, Dewey suggests, that the more complex a society's cultural matrix, the more likely it is to include individuals who possess habits that are informed by differing or even conflicting patterns of social customs (MW14: 90).

The ability of a society's cultural matrix to produce groups with different or even conflicting habits and social customs revealed for Dewey that morality, when taken as defining acceptable parameters of both individual behaviour and behaviour between individuals and groups within society, is also a socially determined activity. Whilst all humans form associations with and are formed by associations (habits/social customs) with natural objects and other human beings within a cultural matrix, it is also the case that all human action has possible consequences for other natural objects and other human beings who share in association or who inhabit the same society:

> Some activity proceeds from a man; then it sets up reaction in the surroundings. Others approve, disapprove, protest, encourage, share and resist... Conduct is always shared; this is the difference between it and a physiological process. It is not an ethical 'ought' that conduct *should* be social. It *is* social, whether bad or good. (MW14: 16)

Importantly, however, Dewey contends that what separates human associations from that of natural objects, such as assemblies of electrons, unions of trees, swarms of insects, herds of sheep or constellations of stars, is the ability of humanity to intelligently perceive, reflect upon and subsequently plan to secure certain consequences and avoid others (LW2: 243, 250, 257). This ability of humans to intelligently perceive the consequences of associated action is structured around two kinds of consequences: those that directly affect individuals engaged in a transaction of associated behaviour and those that indirectly affect individuals beyond those immediately concerned in the transaction.

Within this distinction, Dewey finds the germ of the distinction between conceptions of private and public transactions. Transactions where the consequences of action were confined, or thought to be predominantly confined, to those directly engaged in such associative behaviour are said to be private. Transactions where the consequences are perceived to be extensive, enduring and serious for persons beyond those immediately engaged in such transactions are said to be of a public disposition. However, Dewey refines his position further by stating that this distinction was ultimately drawn on the scope and extent to which consequences were deemed important by a society to warrant control, whether through inhibition or promotion. In essence, all private transactions of associative behaviour have the propensity to become public when they are perceived to have extensive, enduring and serious consequences for others beyond those directly engaged in them. As such, there is no domain of activities that is intrinsically private (LW2: 243–5, 252–3).[9]

It is within the distinction between private and public transactions that Dewey finds the key to the origins of the 'nature and office of the state', arguing that the perception of public transactions leads to emergence of what he calls a 'Public' and subsequently the founding of a state. In Dewey's sense of the term, a public comes into existence when persons, having become conscious of and sufficiently affected by the consequences of associative behaviour (habits) to deem it unacceptable, form a collective group or movement with a common interest in having such consequences systematically controlled or cared for (LW2: 245, cf. 52–3, 260). However, such a public faces a dilemma due to the fact that the very consequences that call forth a public expand beyond those directly engaged in such associative behaviour.

The regulation of such consequences cannot be conducted by the primary groupings involved in the respective associative behaviour in the first place (although self-organization by a group to regulate its activities is also an important phenomenon). Consequently, in organizing themselves to deal with such indirect consequences, such a public creates special agencies and appoints officials such as legislators, judges and executives (which might include members of a public acting as citizens) to regulate behaviour and protect (through laws, rights and establishment of practices) their interests. These officials and special agencies, argues Dewey, are what we nominally call government and help bring forth a state. However, as Dewey is at pains to point out, the state does not solely consist of the inaugurating of government or the rise of a public but rather it is the political organization of the public through government:

> The lasting, extensive and serious consequences of associated activity bring into existence a public. In itself it is unorganised and formless. By means of officials and their special powers it becomes a state. A

public articulated and operating through representative officers is a state; there is no state without a government, but also there is none without a public. (LW2: 277, cf. 245-57, 260)

The central premise of Dewey's conception of the state is its foregoing of any attempt to find the true nature or essence of the state in order to embrace an anti-essentialist view of the state. In this sense, Dewey argues that after the formation of a state through the political organization of a public, its functions (governmental practices, parameters and composition) are themselves prone to changing in character and tone due to the changing historical conditions of associative behaviour and the rise of new publics. In simple terms, Dewey argues that the state possesses a historical relativity of form and function rather than a static and enduring nature.[10]

The reason for this historical relativity of state form and function, Dewey suggests, involved the fact that the consequences of associative behaviour are linked to a society's cultural matrix and the historical propensity for the properties of a society's cultural matrix to change (Dewey, LW2: 263). A cultural matrix, Dewey contends, is itself always open and prone to change due to socio-economic and technological transformation, migration, exploration or wars that modify pre-existing associations or create new associations (habits/customs) and consequences. At the same time, the very perception or meaning attached to the consequences of associated behaviour and the best methods to deal with such consequences can itself shift in terms of a change in intellectual habits. For instance, scientific discoveries or the emergence of a new political paradigm may radically alter how people approach the consequences of associated behaviour (LW2: 263-5, cf. 254-5, 278-9). On the back of this, Dewey stresses that change in a cultural matrix, what we can also call societal change, is a historical fact, which injects perpetual and potentially revolutionary change in multifarious and different marks of intensities across the various relations of associative behaviour within a society (LW11: 41).[11]

As such, Dewey's concept of a public does not denote a static and homogenous body of people but rather plural and ever-changing publics brought into existence in reaction to changes in a society's cultural matrix and the consequences of associated behaviour.[12] On a synchronic level, publics are plural, ranging in size, strength and interests due to the variety of associations, habits and social customs a cultural matrix puts into practice and the perceptions of consequences a cultural matrix provides (LW2: 254–5). For instance, if one considers issues such as animal rights, immigration, homosexuality, women's equality or welfare provision, it is clear that at any one moment in time there are potentially multiple publics with their own agendas and interests, who may or may not support another public's cause.

A person may belong to many different publics, based on how they are subjected to or perceive the consequences of associative behaviour. No two publics are therefore likely to ever have the same membership but a public may possibly possess members from other publics. In turn, because publics are differentiated by the associative behaviour invoked by the contours of material culture, publics may even be constructed in response to other publics. It is quite often the case, for example, that some publics hold interests and ideas of how the state could manage such interests, which other publics may find inherently unreasonable or even dangerous because they conflict with their own interests and values. Consequently, there is, Dewey stresses, often room for dispute or conflict between the interests of differing publics (LW2: 275, 354, cf. LW11: 56).

On a diachronic level, publics also come into existence and pass out of existence in response to the variety of associations a cultural matrix puts into practice and the perceptions of consequences a material culture provides. Publics may not only continue on from and modify the interests from where previous publics left off (e.g. religious/socialist/feminist movements) but may be entirely original movements whose values and interests differ markedly from publics that precede them. All publics, however, emerge within a strategic context where the state and its institutions of government bear the hallmarks of the interests of previous publics. For example, new publics engendered by new conditions in material culture have often found that their inherited institutions, beliefs and traditions of government, which reflect the interests of older publics, suffer from a cultural 'lag' and are unfit to meet their needs (LW2: 255, cf. LW13: 97, LW11: 54, LW12: 82–3).

New publics will therefore often seek to modify the institutions and officials of government to suit their present interests and consequently modify the nature and functions of the state (LW2: 255).[13] This may include fundamentally changing the nature and functions of a state as it has been laid down by previous publics, such as those that founded the state in the first place. In turn, the modification of the state's institutions of government, through changing the nature of associative behaviour and creating new forms of cultural norms and values, will affect and modify a society's cultural matrix and subsequently provide a new cultural matrix (consequences/perceptions of associative behaviour) for the possible emergence of future publics.

In the light of the perpetual propensity of a cultural matrix to change and call forth synchronically and diachronically differentiated publics, Dewey declares that the state is a historically relative entity whose functions were 'ever something to be scrutinized, investigated, and searched for' and hence remade and reorganized in reaction to the conditions of culture (LW2: 255). Dewey sums up his historicist view of the state by propounding that:

> The consequences vary with concrete conditions; hence at one time and place a large measure of state activity may be indicated and at another time a policy of quiescence and *laissez-faire*. Just as publics and states vary with conditions of time and place, so do the concrete functions which should be carried on by states. There is no antecedent universal proposition which can be laid down because of which the functions of a state should be limited or should be expanded. Their scope is something to be critically and experimentally determined. (LW2: 281)

Concluding his examination of the state, Dewey argues that the philosophical preoccupation with an all-encompassing theory of the state's nature had always been a mirage of a goal in the first place. In provisional terms, whilst one could declare that the state was the political organization of the public via government and that such arrangements had certain historical traits of function, ultimately '... what the public may be, what the officials are, how adequately they perform their function, are things we have to go to history to discover' (LW2: 253–6).[14]

The history of publics and the spectre of violence

The qualification that publics, government and consequently the state are historically relative properties based on the movements of a society's cultural matrix is the cornerstone of Dewey's recasting of the meaning of democracy and the justification for its practice vis-à-vis other forms of political settlement. This gambit involves Dewey initially reminding his readers that historical relativity of the state meant examining the formation of statehood and its evolution in the messy reality of human history. Detached from an appreciation of history, it is quite easy to read Dewey's theory of a state being based on a functional logic of publics emerging and progressively altering the institutions and practices of government in response to the changing conditions of culture.

In this schema, the state's evolution would resemble the progressive role set out for it in pluralist philosophy, whereby the state neutrally arbitrated and included the interests of differing publics, who have similar potential and resources for accessing and modifying the formation of government and state functions. Contra pluralism's vision of the state, however, Dewey pointed out that the very history that highlighted that states evolved via changes in the cultural matrix and the rise of publics also brought home the fact that such an evolution did not necessarily guarantee the 'propriety or reasonableness' of the publics or the political acts, measures or systems which emerged from such a process (LW2: 254).

For instance, Dewey highlights that the intellectual foundations (science/political ideologies) of a cultural matrix do not necessarily provide publics or governments with correct or just perceptions about associative behaviour. One has only to think about certain ideologies and subsequent government policies towards women, immigrants, non-whites or homosexuals over the eighteenth, nineteenth and twentieth centuries to see that the observation of the consequences of associated human behaviour is open to the same error and illusion as the perception of natural objects. The emergence of a public can also not be equated with an a priori expression of correctness or justness. As highlighted above, publics can emerge in response to other publics or often come into conflict with one another due to incompatible interests. This process itself can lead to the emergence of illiberal or unreasonable publics. Again, one has only to look to history to find how illiberal publics have shaped unjust state formations or even how what we today would call progressive publics, such as the ones that emerged to demand the abolition of New World Slavery and women's suffrage, were opposed by publics who demanded the status quo or even a heightening of illiberal practices. As a consequence, Dewey contends that mistaken prescriptions, based on such false observations or stemming from the wishes of illiberal publics, can consolidate themselves in laws and administrative policies of government creating retrogressive rather than progressive consequences (LW2: 254).

The historical evidence that culture could facilitate incorrect perceptions of associative behaviour or even invoke illiberal publics served to underline for Dewey that publics have rarely been of equal standing in a society. The historical relativity of the state's form revealed not only that other social groups precede the state, but that the state always exists as a 'distinctive and restricted social interest'— an agency whose form and functions are set up to meet the demands and protect the interests of specific publics within specific cultures at specific junctures in history (LW2: 253–4). For example, although states are brought into existence via the emergence of a public there are often other publics who are excluded from forming government in the very act of founding a state.

This process itself normally reflects socially stratified relations between groups within society at that juncture in history. And whilst the parameters of such social stratification may shift over time due to shifts in power, for example from heredity and lineage to economic class, the power and prestige of government is nearly always held in esteem by dominant groups. Thus, Dewey suggests that the primary task for any public is to achieve such recognition of itself across wider society to give weight to its attempts to modify government and associative behaviour in its interests (LW2: 283). The ability to gain access to the privileges of government has therefore often been distributed through birth into a dominant class, caste, race or gender rather than an ability to govern (LW2: 254, 283–4).[15] This has created circumstances throughout history, where various publics and their interests have found themselves excluded, often unjustly and to their detriment, from the very process of the state being rediscovered and remade.

Moreover, Dewey suggests that well-institutionalized states and their incumbent governments, which reflect the interests and often contain members of previous publics, have historically hindered the process of the remaking of the state. This transpires because the needs of newly formed publics often challenge the moral values or interests of the previous public(s) that have shaped the present state and its government. Subsequently, well-institutionalized incumbent states and their governments have historically used the institutions and practice of government to counteract, discredit or suppress the rival interests of new publics. This expulsion of new publics from partaking in the remaking of the state and government has, Dewey contends, often been the catalyst for violent revolution:

> The new public which is generated remains long inchoate, unorganized, because it cannot use inherited political agencies. The latter, if elaborate and well institutionalized, obstruct the organization of the new public. They prevent that development of new forms of the state which might grow up rapidly were social life more fluid, less precipitated into set political and legal molds. To form itself, the public has to break existing political forms. This is hard to do because these forms are themselves the regular means of instituting change. The public which generated political forms is passing away, but the power and the lust of

possession remains in the hands of the officers and agencies which the dying publics instituted. This is why the change of the form of states is so often effected only by revolution. (LW2: 254–5)

What is of pertinence here is Dewey's belief that the historical relativity of culture and the emergence of new publics translate into a situation where a society is always in a process of transition and hence potential moral conflict. This conflict between the needs of *old experience* and of *new experience*, what we often refer to as *social problems*, is inherently a moral conflict because it concerns what *should be* within a society. Such conflicts, brought about by the events of a shifting cultural matrix, inherently question the values, principles and ends and corresponding social institutions (practices and institutions of government) that should exist at that specific historical juncture (LW13: 151, 184, cf. LW11: 36–7).

All societies, in some form, thus have to come face to face with the dilemma of integrating potentially conflicting moralities of old experience and new experience (Dewey, LW11: 36). However, as the prior notation of the historic propensity of violent revolution makes clear, striking the balance between (or even contemplating integrating the old and the new) has typically been beyond the political wit of humanity. Moreover, Dewey believed that the dilemma of integrating potentially conflicting moralities of old experience and new experience had led some into a belief in the necessity of violent coercive revolution (LW11: 41, 56–61, cf. LW14: 113). On this basis, Dewey concludes that the fundamental problem of political settlement in any society revolves around the question of how to manage social change and mediate potential moral conflict between the old and new experience without the necessity of coercive or violent politics.[16]

Making the case for democracy as a way of life

Rallying against democratic realism's caricature of democracy as merely being a set of defunct institutions, whose failings are only outweighed by the erroneous belief in their ability to succeed in the first place,

Dewey puts forward democracy as the answer to the problem of how to manage societal change and mediate its potential moral conflicts without recourse to coercive or violent politics. In making such a statement, Dewey begins his attempt at deepening, clarifying and ultimately reconstructing the idea of democracy. Although acknowledging the embodiment of the concept in popular suffrage and elected officials, what we commonly call 'political democracy', Dewey contends that the idea of democracy must be separated from its external organs and structure. To reduce democracy to specific institutions or practices is quite simply to miss the fact that democracy is inherently something 'broader and deeper' than such institutions (LW2: 325, cf. LW11: 217 and LW7: 349). This broader and deeper meaning revolves around viewing democracy as the best *method* for establishing and maintaining a society's sense of *community*. And as we shall see, Dewey sees the establishment of community through democracy as paramount to peacefully managing moral conflict as it emerges throughout history (LW11: 56, 182, cf. LW7: 329).[17]

Dewey's reconstructed meaning of democracy is principally exemplified in his demarcation between democracy as a 'way of life' and 'political democracy' as a system of government (LW11: 217, cf. LW2: 325 and LW14: 226). The key to understanding Dewey's conception of democracy as a method for dealing with social change and moral conflict centres around viewing the former as providing the ethical mandate for the constant renewal of the institutions and practices of the latter (LW2: 325, cf. LW11: 182, 218). In its simplest expression, democracy as a way of life represents for Dewey the expression of the democratic ideal or idea (LW7: 348–9, cf. LW2: 327).[18] Underpinned by the Lincolnesque belief that no human is wise enough to rule others without their consent, democracy as a 'way of life' is premised on the necessity for the equal 'participation of every mature being in the formation of the values that regulate the living of men together' (LW11: 217–18, cf. LW13: 294).

The values in question here are the moral values (principles, ends) that justify and inform the social institutions (habits/customs/institutions of the cultural matrix) that influence how individuals both act and relate towards themselves and one another. Within these parameters, democracy as a way of life is best seen as an *ethical commitment* to the principle that those who are affected by social institutions should have a certain share in the production and management of those institutions through contributing to the formation of social policy (proposed reforms of social institutions). Dewey describes this ethical commitment as:

> ... the opportunity, the right and the duty of every individual to form some conviction and to express some conviction regarding his own place in the social order, and the relations of that social order to his own welfare; second, the fact that each individual counts as one and one only on an equality with others, so that the final social will comes about as the cooperative expression of the ideas of many people. (LW13: 295–6).

What is worth noting here is that such an ethical commitment operates on a balanced notion of an equality of participation and communication in the formation of social policy. On one hand, each individual or a group of like-minded individuals who have grouped together (publics) is taken to be equally affected in quality, if not in quantity, by the social institutions under which they live. All individuals or groups of like-minded individuals, regardless of any native (sex) or artificial (race, class, intelligence, political beliefs) endowments, should subsequently have the chance and opportunity to communicate their own conception of moral value. This fundamentally entails an equality of opportunity to express their own needs and desires, their conceptions of how social life should go on and how the social problems they perceive to exist can be solved via reforming social policy. In short, all individuals or groups should have an equality of opportunity to have their moral values solicited and potentially registered in social policy, so as to secure the social institutions that they believe will bring about the full development of their capacities as individuals (LW11: 219–20, cf. LW7: 349–50).

On the other hand, however, this equality of opportunity to contribute to the formation of social policy is balanced by the recognition of the aforementioned social nature of morality. As Dewey points out, '...capacity to endure publicity and communication is the test by which it is decided whether a pretended good is spurious or genuine. Communication, sharing, joint participation are the only actual ways of universalizing the moral law and end' (MW12: 197). The drive for the solicitation and registration of individual or group morality in social policy must always be refracted through the knowledge that such policy will affect and have consequences for 'other' individuals or groups within society, who in all likelihood, due to stratification and different interests engendered by the contours of culture, may share different or competing moral standpoints. The equality of opportunity to express moral value is therefore always used to facilitate the 'mutual conference and consultation' between those groups or individuals who hold differing or competing conceptions of moral value. The overall aim of such mutual conference and consultation is a form of collective problem-solving, where members of society co-operatively collaborate in the appraisal and forming of new social policy in regard to mediating moral conflicts.[19]

In essence, then, the balanced equality of democracy as a way of life and its focus on collective problem-solving highlights Dewey's faith in a deliberative (conference, consultation, negotiation and persuasion) form of political settlement – a process which, Dewey believed, would allow moral conflicts and the resultant social policy decisions to be settled in the 'widest possible contribution of all – or at least the great majority' (LW: 56). However, this deliberative form of political settlement is only able to deal competently with moral conflict both synchronically and diachronically, argues Dewey, because democracy as a way of life facilitates the establishment and maintenance of a society's *community*.

As detailed earlier, just as atoms, stellar masses and cells behave in the natural world, Dewey states that humans within a society directly and unconsciously combine in associated behaviour. Such associated behaviour needs no explanation or meaning; it is simply the way things are structured by culture. The attempt to provide explanation or meaning to associative behaviour and its consequences is for Dewey based on communication, whereby symbols or signs are produced about such associative behaviour and its consequences. The creation of symbols and signs or what we call a common language is thus exactly what publics do when they offer their narrations of associated behaviour and its consequences to wider society. The pivotal point here is that such a process, whereby explanation or meaning is given to associative behaviour and its consequences and then communicated to others, is for Dewey the move towards the establishment of community (LW13: 176).

> A community thus represents an order of energies transmuted into one of meanings which are appreciated and mutually referred by each to every other on the part of those engaged in combined action. 'Force' is not eliminated but is transformed in uses and direction by ideas and sentiments made possible by means and symbols. (LW2: 331)

On this basis, Dewey takes the form of community invoked by democracy as a way of life, what we call the *democratic community*, to be the best means to deal with moral conflict and social problems on both synchronic and diachronic levels. Dewey's idea of the democratic community does not so much do away with moral conflict, which itself is an impossibility, but looks to mediate conflict and avoid violence through facilitating the communicative inclusion of all publics. This is quite simply because the ethical commitment of democracy as a way of life translates into the perpetual maintenance of a community, whereby everyone is afforded an equal opportunity to express moral value and potentially, through deliberation, have that moral value embodied in social policy.

On a synchronic level, as we have seen, due to stratification and the clash of interests that regularly occur between old and new publics, historically new publics have often been cut out of the process of remaking the state and have had to resort to violent revolution to achieve their objectives. Within the remit of the ethical commitment of democracy as a way of life, however, all individuals and groups possess the right to express their moral value. Dewey subsequently believed that the movement towards the necessity of violence to facilitate the changing of the state is largely eradicated under democracy as a way of life because such an ethical commitment aimed:

> ...to bring these conflicts out into the open where their special claims can be seen and appraised, and where they can be discussed and judged in the light of more inclusive interests than are represented by either of them separately... The more the respective claims of the two are publicly and scientifically weighed, the more likely it is that the public interest will be disclosed and be made effective. (LW11: 56)

The democratic way of life and its democratic community also shed light upon Dewey's hopes for a diachronic form of deliberative and co-operative problem-solving to mediate the moral conflicts which are 'bound to arise' in society (LW14: 227–8). Under the tenets of democracy as a way of life, the problematic of facilitating the participation of every mature being in the formation of the values that inform a society's social institutions is never deemed to be permanently solvable, but rather considered a challenge whose demands change across time and space. This is because the ethical commitment that all members of a society will have the chance to voice their moral value and have the potential to inform social policy recognizes the historical relativity of culture and publics – a process where all forms of moral value espoused by new publics, across time and space, would always possess the right to be heard and be deliberated and, if sufficient evidence of its merit emerged, the chance of ultimately changing social policy (LW7: 350). At the heart of the democratic way of life and its sense of community thus beats an educative rhythm, which looks to ensure a perpetual equality of communication and co-operative problem-solving as social conditions and conceptions of moral value shift throughout history.[20]

Democracy as a way of life + political democracy = creative democracy

The question that now remains, however, is how does Dewey's conception of democracy as a way of life relate to what we commonly call political democracy as a system of government? What should be clear from the preceding discussion is Dewey's belief that democracy as a way of life and its sense of community provides the respective ethical and deliberative foundations for the mediation of conflict via facilitating the co-operative reform and remaking of social institutions in response to changing contours of culture and the rise and fall of publics. The interesting point here is that Dewey conceives that democracy as a way of life is not just about political democracy but about the perpetual participation of every mature being in the formation of the values of the social institutions under which they live. As such, Dewey believes that the justification and purpose of the institutions and practices of political democracy are also bound to the democratic way of life.

On one hand, Dewey asserts that the institutions and practices of political democracy should always endeavour to further the pursuit of democracy as a way of life. This means that the institutions and practices of political democracy should endeavour to facilitate the evolution of other social institutions to mediate the changes in culture and conflict between old and new experience. To this end, Dewey contends that the institutions and practices that we commonly associate with political democracy, such as universal suffrage, recurring elections, responsibility of those who are in political power to the voters and the freedom of speech, inquiry and assembly, are the means which have been most expedient at various historical junctures towards the pursuit of the ethical commitment of democracy as a way of life and the upholding of a democratic community (LW11: 218). This is because such institutions and practices of political democracy, through their commitment to equality of discussion, consultation and publicity, are premised on the uncovering and communicating of social needs and troubles and hence facilitate both the ethical mandate of democracy as a way of life and the collective solving of such problems (LW2: 364).

On the other hand, however, the institutions and practices of political democracy are themselves simply social institutions. They are not the final ends or values of democracy as a way of life but rather the mechanisms towards the 'effective operation' of the ideal (LW2: 325).

Against the trend of what he saw as the quasi-religious idealization of political democracy's institutions and practices and other social institutions in general, Dewey argues that we must not see democracy as being 'fixed in its outwards manifestation' (LW11: 182). The institutions and practices of political democracy are not beyond criticism or innovation themselves and are to be appraised on how far they, and the consequences they produce, contribute to the effective operation of the democratic ideal (LW11: 218). For instance, the emergence of moral conflict and the pursuit of deliberatively solving such a problem may uncover that an institution or practice of political democracy is unfit or unsuited to meet the demands of facilitating the democratic way of life in the current contours of culture. Consequently, such defunct institutions and practices of political democracy, just like other social institutions, must be adapted or updated, through deliberative problem-solving, to meet the needs, problems and the conditions of the contemporary configuration of culture (LW11: 182, cf. LW13: 299).

The linkage between democracy as a way of life and political democracy brings home Dewey's conception of 'creative democracy'.[21] Creative democracy is simply shorthand for the working link between the democratic ideal and its outward manifestation in social institutions. For democracy as a way of life is not so much to be statically handed down across generations, argues Dewey, but rather to be inherited and creatively interpreted and enacted anew by each generation and its various publics in regard to their present:

> The very idea of democracy, the meaning of democracy, must be continually explored afresh; it has to be constantly discovered, and rediscovered, remade and reorganized; while the political and economic institutions and social institutions in which it is embodied have to be remade and reorganized to meet the changes that are going on in the development of new needs on the part of human beings and the new resources for satisfying these needs. (LW11: 182)

Dewey concludes that creative democracy, where the democratic ideal is used to structure the evolution of social institutions through mediating the conflict of publics, was the only way to master the changes in social reality both that are already here and that are destined to come forth. Indeed, Dewey saw his approach to democracy as not only potentially radical and revolutionary, but also socially cohesive because of its refusal to ground violence and bloodshed as first principles in the act of being radical and revolutionary. To borrow the words of Dewey's friend and intellectual collaborator George Herbert Mead (1915), this conception of the democratic community was nothing short of the 'institutionalizing of revolution'. This is the sense in which Dewey (LW11: 296) suggests, contra its critics, that 'democracy is radical' and that the 'cure for the ills of democracy is more democracy' (LW2: 325).

Taking in his immediate context, Dewey warned that the choice between creative democracy and other forms of political settlement was stark. He argued that any attempt to merely stand still and not deal with an ever-shifting social reality and ever-changing publics – whether this be through an uncreative and static democracy, a Third Reich, communist utopia or reformulation of philosopher kings as experts – would likely place humanity on the road to extinction. Moreover, as we shall explore in the next chapter, Dewey believed that creative democracy was needed not just within the nation state but beyond and between the nation states of the globe. This was because the violence of revolution had itself been revolutionized, whereby humanity now possessed the unprecedented ability to be the authors of its own collective destruction.

2

The Global Democrat

> *The new era of human relationships in which we live is one marked by mass production for remote markets, by cable and telephone, by cheap printing, by railway and steam navigation. Only geographically did Columbus discover a new world. The actual new world has been generated in the last hundred years.* (LW2: 323)

As the last chapter made clear, John Dewey's conception of creative democracy points towards the perpetual adaption of social institutions, including democratic institutions and practices themselves, as new publics are engendered by social change. In this chapter, I aim to highlight how Dewey's conception of creative democracy was also informed by what he took to be the global interdependence of the Great Society. This centres on how Dewey believed that creative democracy needed to be exercised not only within America, but also outside and between nation states and the various publics engendered and scattered across the globe by what we have come to call the First Great Globalization. To achieve this, the chapter will consist of three sections. The first section highlights the globalized nature of the Great Society by showing how such a time period has today become known as the 'First Great Globalization'. The second section focuses not only on how Dewey acknowledged the global dimensions of the Great Society but also on why he was compelled to propound the need for global democracy. The final part of the chapter outlines Dewey's concrete ideas about what global democracy would look like in reality.

The Great Society as the First Great Globalization

Pragmatist scholars often fail to recognize that Dewey saw the Great Society as more than the radical transformation of the American nation state from an agrarian to a corporate capitalist society.[1] He also saw it as the concomitant radical transformation of the global economy that took place during what has become known as 'the long nineteenth century' (1815–1914). What exactly, then, was this great transformation? Prior to the nineteenth century, there existed a well-defined intercontinental trade system that linked Europe, Asia and the Atlantic colonies of European empires (Findlay and O'Rourke 2007: 365). This had seen world trade grow at 1 per cent per year during the seventeenth and eighteenth centuries. However, as writers such as Frieden (2006), Findlay and O'Rourke (2007) and Rodrik (2011) point out, the long nineteenth century saw the radical transformation of global trade and finance. The transformation of the global economy that took place during the long nineteenth century is now taken to be 'The First Great Globalization'.[2]

The First Great Globalization was driven by historical factors such as the industrial revolution and its new forms of travel (steamships, railways) and communications technology (wireless telegraphs and telephones) that reduced inefficiency and the transaction costs of world trade. Factors such as the hegemonic ascent of free trade ideas as espoused by Smith and Ricardo; the subjection of national macroeconomics to the priorities of the international monetary system of the gold standard; the economic hegemon's (Britain) embrace and upholding of the gold standard; free trade and the consequent export of investment capital by the City of London; the global migration from the Old World to the New World; and European imperialism and the opening up of Asia to free trade combined to create the first genuine integrated world economy. The First Great Globalization thus translated into a scenario in which:

> ... the world economy was essentially open to the movement of people, money, capital and goods. The leading businessmen, politicians, and thinkers of the day regarded an open world economy as the

normal state of affairs. They assumed that people and money would flow around the world with few or no restrictions. Trade protection, although common, was seen as an acceptable departure from the norm, driven by the exigencies of short-term domestic or international politics. Capitalism was global, and the globe was capitalist. (Frieden 2006: 29)

By the mid-nineteenth century, the onset of the First Great Globalization saw world trade grow at a rate of 4 per cent per year for the rest of the century (Rodrik 2011: 24–5). By 1913, every country in Western Europe, bar Spain and Portugal, had industrialized and such developments also took place in countries such as Argentina and Japan. Moreover, a global economic regime emerged across what we today call asymmetric global North and South relations. In this global division of labour, the rich and industrial North, normally under a regime of formal or informal imperialism, exported industrial products in exchange for the primary commodity exports of the poor and largely agricultural South (Findlay and O'Rourke 2007: 402–7, 412–15). Writing in 1919, and over what he perceived as the burning embers of such an order, John Maynard Keynes provides a wonderfully colourful first-hand account of what is meant by the First Great Globalization:

> What an extraordinary episode in the economic progress of man that age was which came to an end in August 1914... The inhabitant of London could order by telephone, sipping his morning tea in bed, the various products of the whole earth, in such quantity as he might see fit, and reasonably expect their early delivery upon his doorstep; he could at the same moment and by the same means adventure his wealth in the natural resources and new enterprises of any quarter of the world, and share, without exertion or even trouble, in their prospective fruits and advantages; or he could decide to couple the security of his fortunes with the good faith of the townspeople of any substantial municipality in any continent that fancy or information might recommend... But, most important of all, he regarded this state of affairs as normal, certain, and permanent, except in the direction of further improvement, and any deviation from it as aberrant, scandalous, and avoidable. The projects and politics of militarism

and imperialism, of racial and cultural rivalries, of monopolies, restrictions, and exclusion, which were to play the serpent to this paradise, were little more than the amusements of his daily newspaper, and appeared to exercise almost no influence at all on the ordinary course of social and economic life, the internationalization of which was nearly complete in practice. (Keynes 1919: 6–7)

As Keynes alludes to above, the long nineteenth century and its globalization was eventually brought to a shuddering halt by the outbreak of the First World War and the rise of trade protectionism that arose from such a global conflict. The period after the war is commonly held to be a period of 'de-globalization' with the onset of 1920s hyperinflation, the Great Depression, trade protectionism and xenophobic nationalism, seeing the world economy split into autarkic economic blocs (Findlay and O'Rourke 2007).[3] However, the evocation of the term 'de-globalization' is slightly misleading as it misses the foolish attempt, between 1925 and 1929, of the developed powers such as Great Britain and the United States to restore the world economy through the re-establishment of the gold standard.[4] As such, even after the war, and in the midst of some trade protectionism and the project of rebuilding Europe, the world's industrial production grew by more than a fifth between 1925 and 1929. And with the rise of American-style mass production and mass consumption, exports swelled to double pre-war levels and world trade became 42 per cent greater in 1929 than in 1913.

This boom was primarily created by the rise of American economic hegemony and Wall Street's usurpation of the City of London as the world's financial centre. Although the United States rejected Britain's political engagement and formal imperialistic underpinning of the long nineteenth century, the rise of American investment capital, taking over from the role of European investment capital, saw over £1 billion a year in loans emanating from New York to foreign destinations between 1919 and 1929. Between 1924 and 1928, America lent on average $500 million per year to Europe, $300 million per year to Latin America, $200 million per year to Canada and $100 million per year to Asia. In tandem, American industrialists and corporations also scoured the globe for foreign direct investment in plants and other ventures. Over the 1920s, American firms invested some $5 billion overseas and saw the rise of multinational corporations such as Ford and General Motors (GM), who became well established in major and minor economies across the globe, and the internationalization of the activities of American commercial banks (Frieden 2006: 140–1, 160–1).

Despite this global economic integration, the reality was that the United States during this period embraced forms of political isolationism in comparison to the international political 'conductor' Great Britain had been when she was the world's pre-eminent economic power. This, of course, was all to lead into the void of the Great Depression and the spread of autarky and ultranationalism. However, the key point is that the ideals of the long nineteenth century and the First Great Globalization still cast a large shadow over the activities of not only America but also the globe post-1914. The question this book seeks to answer is how the casting of such a shadow appeared to John Dewey. As I discuss later, Dewey fully understood that the Great Society was inherently both a national and an international creature.

Dewey's plea for a global Great Community

By 1927, when Dewey wrote *The Public and Its Problems*, he was aware that the First Great Globalization was heavily linked to the problems of publics and the practice of creative democracy within what he called the Great Society. The conception of the Great Society in *The Public and Its Problems* encompasses not only the great transformation of American life but also the global interdependence created by the First Great Globalization. Unfortunately, Deweyan scholars rarely take the global dimensions of the Great Society seriously enough.[5] As a result, what is often missed is how the global dimensions of the Great Society fundamentally informed Dewey's conception of the praxis of creative democracy. Moreover, if read with this understanding in mind, Dewey's political writings from the 1920s onwards can be seen as untangling two intertwined threads concerning the pursuit of democracy as a way of life and the practice of creative democracy within the Great Society.

The first thread, which has been covered by some authors such as Westbrook (1991) and Kadlec (2007), but which has been largely marginalized in other appraisals of Dewey's work, concerns the effects of the Great Society, the rise of democratic realism and the need for democracy as a way of life within America. Nevertheless, Dewey was also aware that much of the complexity and stratification he associated with American corporate capitalism and what he took as the Great Society were engendered by developments of the global economy and the relations between nation states. The second thread, which is even more marginalized than the first in accounts of Dewey's work, recognizes the Great Society not only as an American phenomena but as a state of affairs engendered by what we today call the First Great Globalization and establishes the need for creative democracy at the international level:

> It can be confidently affirmed that every aspect, content, structure and phase of human life has been radically changed, directly or indirectly, for weal or woe, by proliferating and accelerating industrial-technological revolutions. For example: they have changed the structure of family life, the status of women, the relations of the sexes, of parents and children; education has been changed in every respect, quantitatively and qualitatively; vast populations have been urbanized, imposing new occupations and new ways of life; transportation and communication have been revolutionized, with incalculable human consequences; intra-national and international relations, friendly and hostile, cooperative and competitive have been multiplied and intensified; local and world-wide class and race problems have been generated or exacerbated. (LW1: 358)

In *The Public and Its Problems*, Dewey summed this state of affairs up as a 'new era of human relationships' (LW2: 323).[6] Not only did Dewey recognize such unprecedented economic interdependence in and between nation states as the greatest change in human history, but also that such change now created forms of associated behaviour and consequences of associated behaviour that spanned national and continental boundaries. Hence, Dewey believed that the irony of the nineteenth and early twentieth century was that the '...consolation of peoples in enclosed, nominally independent, national states has its counterpart in the fact that their acts affect groups and individuals in other states all over the world' (LW2: 315, cf. LW13: 190).

In *The Public and Its Problems*, the most striking exemplar of the global nature of the Great Society provided by Dewey is the First World War and its aftermath. Dewey begins by highlighting how the war itself was truly global with the involvement of 'every continent upon the globe'. Colonial possessions were drawn in, self-governing nations entered voluntarily and countries with racial and cultural differences, such as Great Britain and Japan and Germany and Turkey, formed alliances. However, the global nature of the conflict aside, Dewey took the First World War to reveal the interdependence of countries in the Great Society and that the consequences of associated behaviour often did not respect national borders. For instance, Dewey highlights how the breakdown of world trade during the war saw a consequent scramble by the belligerents to secure commodities such as raw materials, distant economic markets and foreign capital, which had previously been in abundance due to economic interdependence prior to the war (LW2: 314–17).

At the same time, Dewey saw that the breakdown of such global economic relations created consequences for the everyday life of people across the globe. For example, American farmers, who had experienced temporary prosperity through the increase in demand for agricultural products during the war, saw their economic outlook become bleak when the consequences of the establishment of peace (war debts, the centralization of gold reserves in the United States, depreciations of foreign currencies) meant that wartime levels of export demand declined and failed to return to pre-war levels. Dewey fully acknowledged that the misfortune of American farmers was relatively insignificant in comparison with the other consequences of peace, such as the hyperinflation in Germany and the stimulation of European nationalisms, but it revealed how day-to-day life in one region of the world was now fundamentally linked to, and affected by, the behaviour of others on the far side of the world (LW2: 316).

In essence, the First World War vividly brought home for Dewey how the interdependence of nation states in the Great Society meant the consequences of associative behaviour now spanned across borders. Rather than being a matter of sheer empirical description, however, Dewey found that the case of the American farmer illustrated how little 'prevision and regulation' of such transcontinental interdependence actually existed and how people had as much control over such events as they had over the vicissitudes of the climate (LW2: 316). In 1927, then, the political conclusion he drew from the global nature of the Great Society and the World War it had helped to facilitate was how the existing political and legal institutions and practices were incapable of dealing with the current situation. Contrasting his present with that of Pax Romana, Dewey contended that:

> There was a critical epoch in the history of the world when the Roman Empire assembled in itself the lands and peoples of the Mediterranean basin. The World War stands out as an indubitable proof that what then happened for a region has now happened for the world, only there is now no comprehensive political organization to include the various divided yet interdependent countries. Any one who even partially visualizes the scene has a convincing reminder of the meaning of the Great Society: that it exists, and that it is not integrated. (LW2: 315)

Dewey was all too aware that the reality of globalization now required reform of government that would allow for transnational communication and collaboration and global forms of democratic government. The Great Society needed to become a Great Community which could perfect '… the means and ways of communication of meanings so that genuinely shared interests in the consequences of interdependent activities may inform desire and effort and thereby direct action' (LW2 332, cf. 314, 327).

One can find the same sustained, if not ever-growing, conviction that the Great Society was engendered by modern globalization and lacked political regulation at the international level when one reads elements of Dewey's work through the Great Depression and the rise of trade protectionism, the build-up to the Second World War and in the aftermath of the defeat of the Axis Powers.[7] The intervening years made it clear for Dewey that without a common rule of law and a machinery of government at the international level to manage the effects of the Great Society, the only way nation states knew or sought to deal with the effects of such globalization was economic (autarky, trade protectionism) or military form of warfare (LW11: 261–2).

The *fait accompli* that was the Second World War highlighted for Dewey the '…futility of all thinking, planning and practical effort that is not global in reach' (LW17: 545). Writing in 1944, Dewey outlined again that the Great Society was engendered by the First Great Globalization and had created an interdependent world:

> Commerce, industry, growth of the means of communication between countries physically far apart, did in fact produce interdependence. As Mr. Willkie recently reminded us, we now live in what to all intents and purposes is One World. Distance, the isolating and divisive power of the seas and vast spaces, has been overcome. Steamship and ocean cables began a work which radio and airplane have carried through. For good or bad, we are now and henceforth more like close neighbors in a crowded city than like the widely separate peoples in which our grandparents carried on their affairs in government and industry. (LW17: 453)[8]

Dewey now identified the biggest problem facing the emergence of the Great Community to be the fact that our political beliefs and standards had fallen out of synch with reality. The First Great Globalization had not only brought about physical interdependence across the globe but also engendered a raft of ideas about the teleological advance of democracy, peace and prosperity across the globe. The mistake, Dewey argued, was not the embrace of physical interdependence but the mistaken belief that the breaking down of '…physical barriers, the mere bringing of peoples together into physical contact, would automatically create moral unification' (LW17: 453–4). Humanity was now literally stuck in between 'two worlds' where its political ideas did not match its physical realities:

> One does not have to argue to prove the existence of global physical conditions. It is enough to point to the war in which this country along with almost every country of the globe is engaged. But the fact that it is war which provides the evidence is also proof of absence of moral unification. It points to the nature of the scope, the immensity and the intensity, of the task which lies ahead of us. It points to the futility of all thinking, planning and practical effort that is not global in reach. As yet these things are still largely local, provincial. Politically, our beliefs and standards are nationalistic, not global. (LW17: 454–5)

After the Second World War, Dewey strengthened this line of argument by adding that the war highlighted that the old traditions, customs, habits of belief and institutions of 'old-time diplomacy, power blocs, power politics and precepts of international law' were now as 'outworn and impotent as the old-time muzzle-loading gun' in dealing with the transnational reality of the Great Society. Dewey argued that a world with such interdependence, lacking the means to deal with the effects of such interdependence short of forms of warfare, was essentially a form of 'anarchy'. It was now the 'tragedy of our time' that every person on the planet belonged to a 'world unit' which did not possess a common rule of law and a machinery of government at the international level to manage the international effects of the Great Society (LW15: 204). As such, Dewey declared that:

> ... the responsibility now placed upon us is that of creating the intellectual and moral attitudes that will support institutions, international and domestic, political, educational and cultural, that correspond to the physical revolution which has taken place; and whose consequences are so largely negative just because of the absence of corresponding institutional change. (LW17: 456)[9]

This fact became all the more poignant in the light of the unprecedented destructiveness of the Second World War and the rise of atomic age, which now handed humanity the ability to seemingly wipe itself out of existence (LW1: 358; LW15: 199–202)

Global creative democracy

What, then, of Dewey's concrete ideas about how global democracy could provide governance of the Great Society and how did he think it could be brought into being? Dewey never explained his plans for what such global democracy would look like in a systematic way. Indeed, given his conception of publics amending social institutions in reaction to change and its consequences, such overarching blueprints of global democracy would be somewhat antithetical to Dewey's own idea of creative democracy. However, Dewey as a citizen and public intellectual was also part of publics throughout his life, and his own views of what creative democracy at the global level would look can be teased out from his writings on international affairs. These references to global democracy were not just taken by Dewey as being mere flights of political fancy but based on concrete possibilities in the present.

Dewey's approach to global democracy is essentially two-pronged: it deals with relations between nation states and publics in, and between, those national populations. In the first instance, Dewey's writings in the aftermath of the destruction left by the First World War highlight his belief that the old order of international liberal capitalism, underwritten by imperialism and asymmetric global North/South relations, could be replaced if humanity realized that it was democracy 'for which we are fighting' (MW11: 98–106). Writing in 1918, Dewey argued that peace now brought new problems for social regulation between nation states such as the distribution of labour, immigration and production for export. To subsequently '…annihilate or reduce the agencies of international regulation which already exist …', instead of stabilizing and expanding their scope, Dewey argued, would therefore be 'almost incredible stupidity' (MW11: 130). The world now faced the choice between a return to the status quo of imperialistic rivalry and a new form of global democracy through new institutions of global governance:

> While one can say here as in the case of international relations that a more highly organized world is bound to result, one cannot with assurance say which of the two types of organization is going to prevail. But it is reasonably sure that the solution in one sphere will be congruous with that wrought out in the other. Governmental capitalism will stimulate and be stimulated by the formation of a few large imperialistic organizations which must resort to armament for each to maintain its place within a precarious balance of powers. A federated concert of nations, on the other hand, with appropriate agencies of legislation, judicial procedure and administrative commissions would so relax tension between states as to encourage voluntary groupings all over the world, and thus promote social integration by means of the cooperation of democratically self-governed industrial and vocational groups. (MW11: 105)

Dewey furthered this idea of a new form of global democratic government when he turned his attention to the newly founded League of Nations. In 1918, Dewey saw the League of Nations as a chance to 'end international anarchy' through an embracement of a new form of 'diplomacy', which would displace the elite and aristocratic style of 'old diplomacy' (M11: 132). Despite his eventual disillusionment with post-war international politics, Dewey believed that global democracy required forms of global or international institutions (legislative, judicial, economic) that could regulate the Great Society. These institutions would be pivotal to balance the inequality of power smaller and weaker nations faced from economically and militarily powerful nations and empires (MW11: 139–42).[10]

Dewey did, however, augment his embrace of new international institutions with the notion that to have a 'safe world for democracy' and a world in which democracy was 'anchored' required not only a world-federated government but also the emergence of a 'variety of freely experimenting and freely cooperating self-governing local, cultural and industrial groups' (MW11: 105). This can be seen as Dewey offering a forerunner for ideas of global civil society or the global public sphere. However, by the 1920s, Dewey pushed this argument about the role of public even further. The reformation of the international order towards global democracy was now only possible through both the emergence of a new global architecture of institutions and the 'non-political forces organising themselves to transform existing political structures: that the divided and troubled publics integrate' (LW2: 315).

In order to turn the Great Society into the Great Community, Dewey recognized that the practice of democracy as a way of life needed to be a transnational endeavour, not only between nation-state leaders but also between the various publics scattered across the globe. Reform of democracy between nation states would therefore require transnational communication and collaboration between the peoples of the world and formation of publics that would bring about changes that would bring forth global democracy. This was nothing short of a call for the global inheritance of democracy as a way of life and the rethinking and renewal of the practices and institutions of democracy in the face of the global nature of the Great Society:

> The peoples of the Earth, not just their governmental officials, must find effective answers to the following questions. Is a world-government possible? How shall it be brought into being? By the unilateral and coercive action of some or one nation, or by general cooperative action? What shall be its machinery? What responsibilities shall it possess in order that a common rule of law, expressing the needs of a world-society, may substitute a system of peace and security for the present war system? These questions are urgent; it is imperative to face them at once, directly, and with utmost seriousness. They are not matters of abstract theory but of utmost practical concern. (LW15: 206)

The challenge of 'discovering and implementing politically areas of common interest' between publics and national units in such an interdependent world was now, Dewey decreed, the new political 'imperative' of the twentieth century (LW2: 379). Dewey was himself buoyed by developments after the Second World War. In the second preface to *The Public and Its Problems*, written in 1946, Dewey cited the formation of the United Nations and the opening of debate about the nature of the organization as evidence that there was a growing sense '... that relations between nations are taking on properties that constitute a public and hence call for some measure of political organisation'. Dewey argued that the debate within nation states as to what was 'public' and what was 'private' was being extended into the context of relations between national units. The formation of the UN signalled an acceptance by nation states of the political responsibility that each national unit had towards one another within the Great Community, as opposed to the weak moral responsibility that so easily broke down in the 1930s (LW2: 375–6). And in organizations such as UNESCO Dewey found more evidence that armed conflict was potentially being usurped as the primary method to deal with the effects of globalization. Dewey believed that UNESCO offered '... the peoples of the world a symbol of what is now desirable, and of what may become an actuality' (LW16: 400–1). Yet, as we shall examine in Chapter 3, Dewey's hope that humanity could live up to meeting the challenges of the new imperative of the twentieth century was tempered by what he saw as the eclipse of the public and democracy at home.

The Obstacles to Creative Democracy at Home and Abroad

Only sheer cynicism and defeatism will deny that it is possible to create a workable world government. There have been times when the moral ancestors of present day defeatists would have scornfully declared that a rule of law over a territory anything like as large as our present United States was impossible. They would have said that outside of family groups and small neighbourhoods, the custom of every man's hand against other men could not be uprooted… If peoples, especially their rulers, devoted anything like the energy – physical, intellectual, and moral – that now goes into planning war, to planning for an enduring peace system, they could achieve world government. To surrender to defeatism is for intelligence to abdicate. It is to give up the struggle in a cause in which nothing less than the destiny of civilization is at stake. It is, however, as necessary to appreciate the immense difficulty of the undertaking as it is to have the will to take unreserved part in it. (LW15: 206)

In much the same vein as contemporary advocates of global democracy, Dewey firmly believed that the nature of globalization meant that global forms of democracy were necessary to manage the Great Society. However, Dewey ultimately problematized his own thought when examining the feasibility of global democracy. Writing just after the end of the Second World War, Dewey initially counters 'defeatism' over the ability to govern the globe by reminding his readers that it was once believed that the United States was too big a land mass over which to create rule of law and democracy. Going further, Dewey suggests that if as much thought was put into global democracy as it had been for planning war, it would be more than feasible to create a Great Community and govern the Great Society. However, this optimism towards the project of global democracy is tempered by Dewey's belief that there was an 'immense difficulty' in creating global democracy.

The 'immense difficulty' in the enacting of global democracy was the fact that the Great Society had '… invaded and partially disintegrated the small communities of former times without generating a Great Community' (LW2: 314). As a result, Dewey concludes that the '… new age has no symbols consonant with its activities' and provides no communication of signs and symbols between citizens who are involved in national and transnational associations and consequences engendered by the Great Society. Given the Great Society's technological advancement in communications (telephone, wireless telegraph), the irony of this state of affairs was not lost on Dewey:

> The ties which hold men together in action are numerous, tough and subtle. But they are invisible and intangible. We have the physical tools of communication as never before. The thoughts and aspirations congruous with them are not communicated, and hence are not common…. Our Babel is not one of tongues but of the signs and symbols without which shared experience is impossible. (LW2: 323–4)

This is why, within *The Public and Its Problems*, Dewey pleaded for the 'divided and troubled publics' across not just America but the world to integrate in order to create a Great Community that could bring forth democratic governance at both the national and international level. And this plea is reiterated again in Dewey's work during the Great Depression and in the events that led to the Second World War. Why, then, did Dewey argue that the publics of the Great Society were divided and troubled publics? What was stopping the emergence of a Great Community?

Somewhat expediently, and all too typically in the abstract, Dewey ends the 1946 essay with the answers to such questions when he warns that whilst it was imperative to 'begin' the path towards global democracy it was important to recognize that:

As has been only too proved by the two devastating world wars the movement toward production of more comprehensive social organisation, the very movement that brought national states into being has been widely arrested. (LW15: 209)

When taken with Dewey's conception of democracy in mind, it becomes clear that the forestalling of the emergence of a Great Community was not down to any spatial-temporal limits on the practice of democracy, but rather resulted from what Dewey saw as the arresting of creative democracy and the democratic community at the level of the nation state. The arresting of creative democracy and its ability to update the practices and institutions of democracy were forestalling the 'production of more comprehensive social organization' not only within the nation state but also outside the nation state. Of course, this answer itself begs the questions: What did Dewey take to be the reason for the arresting of creative democracy within the nation state? And how did this arresting of creative democracy within the nation state impact on the cause of global democracy?

The eclipse of the public

The answers Dewey provides to the questions above see him initially outdo democratic realism at its own game. In superficial agreement with democratic realism, Dewey argued that it was the complexity of the Great Society, which had led to the 'eclipse' of publics and a sense of community within nation states and the subsequent arresting of creative democracy. This had transpired because the Great Society's multiplication, intensification and trans-nationalization of associative behaviour now outstripped the comprehension and knowledge of average citizens (LW2: 314–17). The age when citizens could adopt a few general political principles, such as embracing states' rights vis-à-vis centralized federal government or free trade vis-à-vis protectionism, and apply them with confidence through supporting one political party over another was now essentially over. Citing the example of the problem of industrial tariffs, Dewey explained,

> For the average voter today the tariff question is a complicated medley of indefinite detail, schedules of rates specific and *ad valorem* on countless things, many of which he does not recognize by name, and with respect to which he can form no judgment. Probably not one voter in a thousand even reads the scores of pages in which rates of toll are enumerated and he would not be much wiser if he did. The average man gives it up as a bad job. (LW2: 317)

Due to the fact that modern industry was 'too complex and intricate', citizens were essentially 'bewildered' by the machinations of the Great Society. Unable to correctly locate where the indirect consequences that were affecting their daily lives came from, citizens could now not generate publics who could foster the reform of the social institutions of the state to control and regulate such consequences:

> An inchoate public is capable of organization only when indirect consequences are perceived, and when it is possible to project agencies which order their occurrence. At present, many consequences are felt rather than perceived; they are suffered, but they cannot be said to be known, for they are not, by those who experience them, referred to their origins. It goes, then, without saying that agencies are not established which canalize the streams of social action and thereby regulate them. Hence the publics are amorphous and unarticulated. (LW2: 317)

At first glance, one may find Dewey's account of what he took to be the eclipse of publics as not too dissimilar to the view of democratic realism. In fact, Dewey appears to hold the same conviction as Walter Lippmann when highlighting how the voting public struggled to cope intellectually with the complex manoeuvrings of the Great Society. However, whilst both Dewey and democratic realism locate the 'intelligence' of the masses as a key reason for the stuttering of democracy, they radically differ on what they believe were the reasons for such a state of affairs. Democratic realism took it to be the case that the masses were a priori incapable of ever grasping the contours of the Great Society because it was too complex and demanded expert rule. Dewey, on the other hand, saw the lost nature of the public and the collapse of democracy to be down to wholly contingent reasons that limited the intelligence of the masses.

Primarily, Dewey identified the limiting of the public's intelligence and subsequent eclipse as being a result of the fact that modern liberal democracy within the Great Society had only achieved 'bourgeois democracy' rather than actual creative democracy. The historic emergence of liberal democratic governments in the nineteenth century 'had been an accompaniment of the transfer of power from agrarian interests to industrial and commercial interests'. Whilst there had been a change in the social order, with the rise of democratic government and the handing of power to industrial and commercial interests, the ability to '... command the conditions under which the mass of people have access to the means of production and to the products of their activity...' continued to give 'power to the few over the many'. The reality was that in liberal bourgeois democracies, power lay in the hands of 'finance capitalism', no matter the claims of so-called governments *of*, *by* and *for* all the people. And whilst Dewey freely admitted that it would be 'silly' to deny that there had been great gain for the masses within liberal democracies, such as qualified suffrage, freedom of speech, press and assembly, he also viewed it as intellectual hypocrisy to 'glorify these gains and give no attention to the brutalities and inequities, the regimentation and suppression' which plagued the system of economic liberalism (LW11: 296–7).

This was no understatement. Although US society in the 1920s was one of apparent prosperity, it was still marked by severe racist segregation, economic inequality, regressive income tax, precarious employment, lack of industrial democracy and a relatively non-existent welfare state. By the time of the Great Depression, when such material inequality and the lack of means to deal with such conditions became even more acute, Dewey lamented that there were now 'millions of people who have the minimum of control over the conditions of their own subsistence' (LW13: 300).¹ Yet, as Dewey pointed out, 'no economic state of affairs is merely economic' (LW11: 295). The most unjust and immoral aspect of such an unequal economic state of affairs was the role they played in the eclipse of the public and the stunting of creative democracy:

> The same forces which have brought about the forms of democratic government, general suffrage, executives and legislators chosen by majority vote, have also brought about conditions which halt the social and humane ideals that demand the utilization of government as the genuine instrumentality of an inclusive and fraternally associated public. (LW2: 303)

The halting of the social and humane ideals Dewey associated with creative democracy was inherently down to bourgeois democracy being founded on the idea that laissez-faire capitalism was the true expression of human liberty. This had arisen, Dewey stressed, because in the fight against arbitrary government action and for religious freedom, mid-nineteenth century philosophical branches of liberalism had identified the 'immutable truth' that human liberty was to be found in the practices of laissez-faire capitalism. In this sense, human nature and natural law could be said to be fulfilled when liberty was perceived as the equal right of every individual to conduct economic enterprise free from government constraint, so long as they broke no law on the statute books. This, in turn, was said to be socially beneficial because the activities of self-interested individuals would automatically create competition that would provide socially needed commodities and services. Any government intervention that interfered with this form of liberty was to be taken as an attack on liberty itself. This conception of liberty, which was presented by eighteenth and nineteenth-century liberals – from Adam Smith to Mill – as an 'immutable truth' across time and space, was ultimately used by the commercial and industrial classes to firstly usurp the vested interests of mercantilism and then serve as the hegemonic justification for bourgeois democracy (LW11: 26–7, cf. LW2: 291–3).²

Dewey found that the hegemonic perpetuation of the ideal that laissez-faire capitalism equalled the 'philosophy of liberty' had had a profound impact upon the intelligence of the masses and the subsequent eclipse of the public. By the 1930s, it was apparent that laissez-faire capitalism and its conception of liberty had delivered extreme stratification rather than the liberty of all. However, defenders of the status quo, such as commercial and industrial interests who benefited from these conditions and philosophies as social Darwinism, argued that the supposed natural inequalities of individuals in moral and intellectual make-up not only explained economic inequality but were the consequences of natural law. Against the failure of those who were naturally deficient in being innovative, independent and economically proactive stood the success of those 'rugged individuals' who managed to practise liberty and gain wealth and property (LW11: 286–7).

Defenders of the status quo again argued that any government intervention interfered with this form of liberty was therefore to be taken as an attack on liberty itself. Such arguments were indicative to Dewey of how, within the confines of bourgeois democracy, the very concept of intelligence itself had fallen under the strictures of laissez-faire capitalism. However, as he reminded his readers, this simply reflected the failure of modern proponents of liberalism and industrial and commercial interests to recognize, or admit, that individuals were formed by the interaction of the human organism with its environment, and how the current economic regime affected such interaction (LW11: 29–32, 47–8, 286).

In this sense, *'effective* intelligence' was not an 'original, innate endowment'. No matter the differences in native intelligence between individuals, the reality was that the 'actuality of mind' was deposited by social habits and customs (LW2: 366). Rallying against apologists of both laissez-faire capitalism and democratic realism, Dewey highlighted how economic relationships and hegemonic ideals of bourgeois democracy worked in tandem to limit the access of the masses to information and educative practices that could bolster their intelligence. The majority engaged in the production and distribution of economic commodities, argued Dewey, have '... no share – imaginative, intellectual, emotional – in directing the activities in which they physically participate' (LW5: 104). The strictures of industrial and economic relations within the Great Society, such as the mass-production techniques of Fordism, meant that individuals tended to 'become cogs in the vast machine whose workings they do not understand, and in whose management they have no part or lot in' (LW11: 252).

However, Dewey's use of the term 'cogs' needs to be clarified because it does not simply translate into a belief that the masses had regressed and become less advanced humans in the Great Society. On the contrary, reflecting on the new habits of knowledge and industry in 1927, for example, Dewey highlighted how present-day citizens could, due to education and a relative popularizing of science, talk about and understand science in ways far more complex than their predecessors:

> Capacities are limited by the objects and tools at hand. They are still more dependent upon the prevailing habits of attention and interest which are set by tradition and institutional customs. Meanings run in the channels formed by instrumentalities of which, in the end, language, the vehicle of thought as well of communication, is the most important. A mechanic can discourse ohms and amperes as Sir Isaac Newton could not in his day. Many a man who has tinkered with radios can judge of things which Faraday did not dream of. It is aside from the point to say that if Newton and Faraday were now here, the amateur and mechanic would be infants besides them. The retort only brings out the point: the difference made by different objects to think of and by different meanings in circulation. A more intelligent state of social affairs, one more informed with knowledge, more directed by intelligence, would not improve original endowments one whit, but it would raise the level upon which the intelligence of all operates. The height of this level is much more important for judgment of public concerns than are differences in intelligence quotients. (LW2: 366)

Contra democratic realism, Dewey held that citizens could, through improving education and media practices and forging a greater involvement in industry and politics, develop habits that would allow them to act more intelligently without necessarily making them 'omnicompetent' or improving their native levels of intelligence. The proof itself was already apparent in the skill and knowledge of the amateur and mechanic compared to that of Newton and Faraday. The struggle of masses to adequately judge public matters within the Great Society transpired because of a lack of habits rather than inability of the masses to ever master such habits.

Dewey argued that this lack of emphasis on developing the mind of the masses could also be found in the wider public education policies of liberal democracies, which failed to provide the masses with the knowledge they needed in order to make correct judgements about the nature of the Great Society they inhabited. The public school system merely reproduced the hegemony of laissez-faire capitalism and its conception of liberty. For example, between 1929 and 1935, 12 million Americans had reached the employment age and at least half had not found steady employment as a result of the Great Depression. What Dewey found equally appalling was how public education had ill-equipped young people to comprehend the Great Society and had perpetuated the so-called merits of laissez-faire capitalism:

> It is terrible enough that so many youths should have no opportunity to obtain employment under the conditions set by the present economic system. It is equally terrible that so many young people should be refused opportunity in what we *call* a public educational system, to find out about the causes of the tragic situation, and, in large measure, should be indoctrinated in ideas to which the realities about them give the lie. Confusion and bewilderment are sufficiently rife so that it is not necessary to add to them a deliberately cultivated blindness. (LW11: 354)

Added to the intellectual hegemony of stratification, Dewey believed that technological innovation and subsequent integration into consumer capitalism also affected the ability of the public to comprehend their present circumstances. This largely concerned the nature of the new media technologies and their integration into mass production and mass consumption. Man after all, Dewey contended, was a 'consuming and sportive animal as well as a political one', and the power of 'bread and circuses' to distract citizens from political concerns was nothing new. But he took the sheer number and variety of modern cheap consumer products, such as the 'movie, radio, cheap reading matter and motor car', as a wholly unprecedented scenario of political distraction:

> In most circles it is hard work to sustain conversation on a political theme; and once initiated, it is quickly dismissed with a yawn. Let there be introduced the topic of the mechanism and accomplishment of various makes of motor cars or the respective merits of actresses, and the dialogue goes on at a lively pace. The thing to be remembered is that this cheapened and multiplied access to amusement is the product of the machine age, intensified by the business tradition which causes provision of means for an enjoyable passing of time to be one of the most profitable of occupations. (LW2: 321–2)

Although Dewey did not hold that such modern media technologies and products had been purposefully created as a culture industry, the fact that they did not originate in deliberate desire to divert political interest did not lessen their effectiveness in that direction (LW2: 321). The use of modern technology and mass-production techniques to create mass consumer products thus lead to forms of mass consumption that often distracted citizens from political issues.[3]

When Dewey examined how new media technologies, such as the 'telegraph, telephone, radio, cheap and quick mails', impacted upon the dissemination of information as 'news' to the public, he saw even more cause for concern. News, as Dewey stated,

> ... signifies something which has just happened, and which is new just because it deviates from the old and regular. But its *meaning* depends upon relation to what it imports, to what its social consequences are. This import cannot be determined unless the new is placed in relation to the old, to what has happened and been integrated into the course of events. Without coordination and consecutiveness, events are not events, but mere occurrences, intrusions; an event implies that out of which a happening proceeds. (LW2: 347)

The problem Dewey found with news coverage was that it centred on triviality and sensationalism. Driven by the 'catastrophic, namely crime, accident, family rows, personal clashes and conflicts,' such news coverage did not supply continuity of coverage to its audiences but rather supplied whatever would be taken as the 'new par excellence'. As a result, Dewey quipped that the contents of news coverage became so interchangeable that only the 'date of the newspaper' could inform us whether such events happened 'last year or this, so completely are they isolated from their connections' (LW2: 346–7).

The explanation of this state of affairs, argued Dewey, was also down to the mixing of business practices and interests with modern media technology. Bourgeois democracy's 'quasi-democratic' habits of free speech, free press and free assembly created fertile ground for different sources of news production and public discussion. However, such freedoms were structurally prone to being undermined by the fact that the centralization and concentration of the means of production and distribution also had concomitant effects upon the organization of the public press. As Dewey noted, the smoothest road to control of political matters was through the construction of public opinion, and it was no coincidence that the gathering and sale of news had become part of the existing system of 'pecuniary profit' (LW2: 348–9). This resulted in not only the influence of 'private interests in procuring suppression, secrecy and misrepresentation,' but also the importing of the hegemony of consumer capitalism into news production and dissemination. This was what Dewey took as the explanation for the sensationalist and triviality of what passed for news. Thus, either through the perpetuation of a certain style of consumer capitalism in news production and dissemination or through direct ownership and influence, Dewey believed that large corporate capitalism naturally influenced the publishing business (LW13: 168).

Contra the arguments of democratic realism and defenders of the laissez-faire capitalism, Dewey argued that the eclipse of the public was not down to its innate intellectual deficiency but largely down to the artificial intellectual inequality engendered by bourgeois democracy and elements of its consumer culture:

> The indictments that are drawn against intelligence of individuals are in truth indictments of a social order that does not permit the average individual to have access to the rich store of the accumulated wealth of mankind in knowledge, ideas and purposes. There does not now exist the kind of social organization that even permits the average human being to share the potentially available social intelligence. Still less is there a social order that has for one of its chief purposes the establishment of conditions that will move the mass of individuals to appropriate and use what is at hand. Back of the appropriation by the few of the material resources of society lies the appropriation by the few in behalf of their own ends of the cultural, the spiritual, resources that are the product not of the individuals who have taken possession but of the cooperative work of humanity. (LW11: 38–9)

It was therefore useless, Dewey lamented, to ruminate about the apparent failure of democracy until the sources of its failure had been grasped and steps were taken, namely using government action to address such economic and intellectual inequality, to bring about that type of social organization that would deliver the masses with the correct knowledge to comprehend the Great Society and practise creative democracy. Quite simply, Dewey argued, without enacting such a change we 'have no way of telling how the apt for judgment of social policies the existing intelligence of the masses may be' (LW2: 366).[4]

The national and global eclipse of creative democracy

The effects of the eclipse of the public meant that creative democracy at the level of the nation state had essentially been eclipsed. Not only did ordinary citizens have no real democratic control over the Great Society at the national level, but also publics were not able to emerge and articulate demands that could generate the reform of social institutions in the first place. Dewey realized that the eclipse of the public allowed the regime of 'bourgeois democracy' to continue to underpin the institutions and practices of political democracy at the nation state level. Due to the fact that democratic government had arisen along side laissez-faire ideas of liberty, capitalism and the practice of democracy were now seen as 'Siamese' twins, where to attack one was to threaten the life of the other (LW13: 137). Indeed, Dewey took the example of the application of laissez-faire to individual intelligence to be indicative of how liberalism's tenets had become part of a wider political malaise within political democracy, which now acted as 'an instrument of vested interests' (LW11: 35).

This in turn had a pincer effect on the nature of political democracy under bourgeois democracy and its perpetuation of the eclipse of the public. On one hand, Dewey argued that in the 1920s and 1930s political parties ruled but they did not govern, acting as quasi 'servants of the same dominant railway, banking, and corporate industrial forces' (LW6: 186, cf. LW5: 442). This was not just through blatant corrupt control of government, but rather because the hegemonic identification of capitalism and democracy and the ability of business to actually organize itself as a public meant that it was able to reform the state and government in much the same way as 'dynastic interests' controlled government two centuries earlier (LW2: 302). In the inevitable clash between private property interests and the interests of the masses, all the 'habits of thought and action' impelled the institutions of political democracy to side with the former over the latter (LW6: 159).

On the other hand, the fact that political parties acted in the interests of capital rather than people had significant impact on the actual eclipse of the public. Government intervention on the effects of such an economically and intellectually stratified society was always palliative and dealt with symptoms rather than what Dewey took as the causes of such a state of affairs. This, in turn, locked the masses into the perpetual supporting of one impotent political party over the other, breeding a swing-style democracy where the 'tidal wave' swamps one party and the 'landslide' carries the other into office. In such a form of politics, instead of real policy difference, it was rather 'habit, party funds, the skill of managers of the machine, the portrait of the candidate with his firm jaw, his lovely wife and children, and a multitude of other irrelevancies' determined the outcome of political democracy (LW2: 311).

The impotency of existing political forms to direct and manage the social effects of the Great Society was also now generating 'distrust in political democracy and all forms of popular government' (LW13: 105–6). This was because political democracy, with its established institutions and practices under the hegemonic control of laissez-faire capitalism, had seen its 'symbols lose connection with the realities behind them' (LW11: 51). The majority of the voting public convinced that there was 'no important difference between the two old parties' and that to vote for one over the other was to signify very 'little' had lost faith with democracy (LW6: 185). Not only did this further add to the political apathy engendered in the majority under the auspices of bourgeois democracy and its consumer culture, but with such public apathy, political democracy itself became stratified and turned into just another 'business' run by the 'bosses' and 'managers' of the 'political machine'. Political democracy was thus now left to the machinations of professional politicians and elites, who rather than attempting to serve the public looked to keep or obtain power for the sake of keeping or obtaining power within the confines of bourgeois democracy (LW2: 321, LW7: 353–4).

The ultimate political effect of the eclipse of the public within the nation state was destruction of the Deweyan sense of democratic community and disharmony within the nation state. This point is pivotal; whilst Dewey believed citizens were unable to correctly locate where the indirect consequences that were affecting their daily lives came from, and hence could not generate publics which could foster the reform of social institutions of the state to control and regulate the consequences of the Great Society, he did not believe that citizens could no longer generate publics. As he pointed out,

> It is not that there is no public, no large body of persons having a common interest in the consequences of social transactions. There is too much public, a public too diffused and scattered and too

intricate in composition. And there are too many publics, for conjoint actions which have indirect, serious, and enduring consequences are multitudinous beyond comparison, and each one of them crosses the others and generates its own group of persons especially affected with little to hold these different publics together in an integrated whole. (LW2: 320)

The irony of the Great Society was that the more it made citizens more interdependent through its division of labour and production, the more it seemed to create divisions of interest between various groups across society. In fact, due to the inequality and stratification of bourgeois democracy, Dewey saw that groups and their publics referred back to an approach of being antagonistic and hostile towards one another, rather than democratically addressing the cause of their dissatisfactions. The emergence 'in political life of populist movements, square deals, new deals, accompanies depressions on the part of those most directly affected – farmers, factory labourers –' was indicative of how such groups were kept from 'uniting politically by divergence of immediate interests' (LW13: 106). Under bourgeois democracy, then, the educative rhythm of creative democracy, which looks to ensure a perpetual equality of communication and co-operative problem-solving as social conditions and conceptions of moral value shift throughout history, was non-existent.

Stuck with old and outdated social institutions, a form of democracy that was actually not democratic, and an eclipse of the public and community which could bring reform to such social institutions, creative democracy was thus stunted at the nation state level. Political democracy in America was a prime example of this process, where the state had not reformed its social institutions, such as wider and reformed education, workplace democracy and comprehensive unemployment insurance, and was now unable to deal with the consequences of the Great Society. Indeed, the American institutions and practices of political democracy themselves had not been updated and struggled to cope with the new demands placed upon them. As Dewey noted, whilst Americans had inherited the local town hall meetings of their agrarian forefathers, these practices were now insufficient to enact reforms suitable for 'national affairs – now also affected by world conditions' (LW13: 95, cf. LW2: 306).

Even at the federal level, the success of industrial forces in controlling political parties had locked in what Dewey viewed as a flawed system of two-party adversarial politics. The idea that the conflict between political parties would bring out 'public truths', stressed Dewey, was a kind of 'political watered down version of the Hegelian dialectic, with its synthesis arrived at by a union of antithetical conceptions' (LW11: 51). And whether it was the 'rugged individualism' of the Hoover regime or the 'piecemeal policies undertaken ad hoc' of Roosevelt's New Deal, which whilst seeming radical did not really reform the 'institutional scheme of things', political democracy merely 'drifted' along, largely consolidating the economic and intellectual stratification of bourgeois democracy (LW11: 45, 61–2, cf. LW13: 315). The result, as Dewey observed, was that the Great Society and its new age of human relationships had 'no political agencies worthy of it' (LW2: 303).

It has become the norm to read Dewey's account of the eclipse of the public and the stunting of creative democracy as simply being concerned with the American nation state. However, there is no doubt that Dewey's claim that the Great Society had no political agencies worthy of it extended to matters of global democracy. As outlined above, one of the underlying themes of *The Public and Its Problems* and his writings thereafter is of the need for the Great Society to become a Great Community. And Dewey knew that the Great Society did not just stretch across North America but rather traversed the world's continents. That such an international Great Community and global democracy was not forthcoming due to the eclipse of the public was also paramount in Dewey's mind. Writing in 1939, Dewey reflected on how, since the First World War, the 'world communities' had failed to 'meet and forestall' needed change and left 'us with old problems unsolved and new ones added' (LW13: 316).

Dewey held that the failure to initiate such change was undoubtedly down to the fact that bourgeois democracy and the breakdown of creative democracy within the nation state made such change improbable. This was down to two interrelated reasons. The first reason was that the hegemony of bourgeois democracy always meant that political leaders would attempt palliative measures that maintained the hegemony of capitalism and its conception of liberty. We have seen how this strangled the reform that Dewey thought was needed at the level of the nation state. However, bourgeois democracy's control of the Great Society was not only based on domestically stratified societies in the West, but functioned through a global economy based on asymmetric relations between the global North and South. As a basic provision of global democracy, the wretched of the earth would have been set free from the shackles of imperialism and the whole of the global economy would have restructured (MW11: 139–42). This, however, was unforthcoming as leaders replicated their palliative measures that maintained the hegemony of capitalism and its conception of liberty in the global economy.

The second reason was that the eclipse of the public meant citizens were in no position to demand their leaders enact such changes. In fact, the consequences of the Great Society and the eclipse of the public and community at the nation state undoubtedly had detrimental effects on how nation states viewed and conducted international relations towards one another. As Dewey noted in *The Public and Its Problems*, throughout history man has had problems getting on with his fellows, even in his neighbourhood. With the Great Society's engendering of the transnational forms of relationships and interdependence, Dewey noted that man was not now 'more successful' in getting on with his fellows 'when they act at a great distance in ways invisible to him' (LW2: 317). The subsequent problem of there being too many publics who were 'diffused and scattered and too intricate in composition', who were subsequently antagonistic towards one another, was therefore not confined to groups within the nation states, but also extended to publics between nation states.

As the 1930s had shown, antagonism towards citizens of other nation states, either through outright fascism or ideals of isolationism, could be seen to be one of the last points of unity that the divided and troubled publics of nation states had left. It was therefore no surprise to Dewey that the failure of world communities to meet and forestall the failings of bourgeois democracy and regulate the transnational consequences generated by the Great Society through creative democracy at home and abroad had seen the growth of 'exacerbated Nationalism' and left democracy both as an ideal and as a form of government under attack from both the 'right and left' (LW13: 106, 316). As Dewey noted,

> The career of individuals, their lives and security as well as prosperity is now affected by events on the other side of the world. The forces back of these events he cannot touch or influence – save perhaps by joining in a war of nations against nations. For we seem to live in a world in which nations try to deal with the problems created by the new situation by drawing more and more into themselves, by more and more extreme assertions of independent nationalist sovereignty, while everything they do in the direction of autarky leads to ever closer mixture with other nations – but in war. (LW13: 180)

The rise of fascism and hyper-nationalism was the exemplar of this process and was essentially explained by the inequality and stratification of bourgeois democracy and its inability to provide citizens with the intellectual and political means of perceiving and controlling the consequences generated by the Great Society. Dewey saw the success of fascist movements as being down to their ability to fill the political void citizens experienced in bourgeois democracy by momentarily appearing to offer an explanation and political solution to the drastic changes engendered by living in such an interdependent world. Of course, such explanations and political solutions were a mirage that led to totalitarianism. Rather than creating a community in Dewey's sense, such movements attempted to restore a simulacrum of a community, such as *völksgemeinschaft*, that were hostile not only to bourgeois democracy but also to the ideals of creative democracy and the Great Community (LW13: 176, 315–16).[5]

This was the scenario Dewey feared most when considering the future of global democracy: the eclipse of the public in nation states and the consequences engendered by the Great Society leading citizens to turn away from forming a Great Community and turning upon one another. This view is summed up when, in the midst of the Great Depression, trade protectionism and the increasing threat of another world war, Dewey castigates the hostility of not only fascism, but also the eclipsed publics contained within bourgeois democracies towards the ideals of global democracy and a Great Community:

> We cannot blame our Government or any other government for not instituting new policies as long as the peoples themselves are engaged in the futile task of identifying patriotism with isolation, and trying to obtain independence without regard to the interdependence that now exists. It is for us, the people, first to develop a genuine cooperative spirit and sense of mutual interests that bind the nations of the world together for weal or woe – and at the present time so largely for woe. The principle of good neighborliness is as fundamental in international matters as in the village and city... We shall refuse to live up to it at our peril, the peril of depression, unemployment, degraded standard of living, and of war that will kill millions more and destroy billions more of property. (LW11: 263–4)

Dewey believed that this call for a new generation to inherit democracy as a way of life and reinvent democracy globally was a responsibility that the world could not afford to turn its backs on. However, Dewey's underlying point was that this inheritance could not be claimed under the auspices of bourgeois democracy. It was thus bourgeois democracy and the Great Society's engendering of 'divided and troubled publics' within and between nation states and the breakdown of creative democracy at the nation state level that Dewey saw as the 'immense difficulty' facing global democracy. Without informed and educated publics who could comprehend the complexity and trans-national nature of the Great Society, communicate transitionally and challenge the hegemony of bourgeois democracy, there was simply no chance of real democratic innovation at home or abroad. Put simply, until the Great Society was converted into a Great Community, the public would perpetually remain eclipsed (LW2: 324).

4

Social Intelligence and Equality

> *The democratic faith in human equality is belief that every human being, independent of the quantity or range of his personal endowment, has the right to equal opportunity with every other person for development of whatever gifts he has.* (LW14: 227)

> *We talk a great deal about democracy as equality of opportunity and then we adopt a system of private ownership of opportunities that makes our boast a farce and a tragedy.* (LW11: 256)

Throughout his life and beyond it, Dewey's work on creative democracy has largely been criticized as being complicit with capitalism or being toothless in its opposition to capitalism. We have already seen that Bertrand Russell (1922) and Lewis Mumford (1926) argued that pragmatism was an expression of the material excesses of American capitalism and the Gilded Age. The Frankfurt School would echo similar critiques of the complicity between Dewey, his fellow classical pragmatists and the capitalist social order (Lukacs 1971; Horkheimer 1972; Adorno 1973). Reinhold Niebuhr (1932) would label Dewey as a politically apathetic thinker, who had lurched towards believing in the idea of a self-correcting form of reason – a thought rearticulated by C. Wright Mills in the 1960s when he would declare that Dewey's work lacked an account of the power structures of the modern capitalist social order (Mills 1964). Even sympathetic interlocutors like Robert Westbrook (1991, 2005), Michael Eldridge (1998) and Cornel West (1989) appear to suggest that Dewey provided far too few concrete practical means to achieve his own democratic ends. As Richard Bernstein (2010: 87) puts it, Dewey's idea of democracy as way of life argues for a 'social goal based on an inclusive plan' but fails to spell out the details of such an 'inclusive plan'.[1]

Both sets of these claims seem to miss the mark. As we have seen, Dewey certainly was no apologist for liberal capitalism at home or abroad. And whilst Dewey was often unforthcoming or rather unwilling to offer definitive blueprints for how to achieve creative democracy, it is also unfair to say that Dewey left behind few concrete practical means to achieve his own democratic ends. Dewey thought that the collapse of European democracy into totalitarianism and the eclipse of the public in America transpired because democratic habits were no longer part of the 'bone and blood of the people in daily conduct of its life'. To this end, Dewey put forward a whole raft of reforms that he believed would help democracy as a way of life become part of the 'fibre' of the people (LW11: 225). These included reforms such as new approaches to the American economy, public education, the role of social science and the social scientist as an 'expert', media regulation and the role of the arts in democracy.[2]

All of these concrete proposals deserve attention and serve as an example of how Dewey believed reforms could bring forth a greater array of democratic habits that would facilitate the practice of creative democracy. However, for the purposes of our exposition of a 'global' Dewey, in this and the next chapter, I want to focus on the concrete lessons Dewey put forward on how to achieve democracy at home and abroad and how both spheres of democracy were intertwined. In this chapter, I specifically want to focus on Dewey's ideas about the economic reforms needed to facilitate what he called social intelligence in the midst of a liberal-capitalist order that stunted the intelligence of its citizens. Moreover, I want to focus on Dewey's ideas about how the Great Society and its regime of bourgeois democracy needed to shift to a form of democratic socialism to achieve the goal of becoming a Great Community. These economic reforms not only seemingly laid the grounds for all of Dewey's other reforms but were also based on the need to provide the ethical commitment at the heart of democracy as a way of life and the grounds for an expanded social intelligence both within and beyond the nation state. This chapter will therefore outline how Dewey believed that the Great Society was to be regulated not only to avoid the mutual destruction of humanity but also to succeed in harnessing 'available human energy' (LW13: 312).

To illustrate the above, the chapter will proceed through four movements of argument. The first section will outline how Dewey's idea of creative democracy was based upon a form of deliberation he called social intelligence and how social intelligence is essentially an adoption of the 'scientific attitude of the mind' in moral and political matters. The second section will outline how Dewey believed liberal capitalism was unable to support social intelligence and needed replacing with a form of democratic socialism. The third section will outline how Dewey's call for democratic socialism was animated by his view about the relationship between economic inequality and political equality within the Great Society. The final section will highlight how Dewey's views on economic and political equality translate into an argument for an extension of global egalitarianism that would allow all nations of the world to pursue the democratic way of life.

The habits of social intelligence

As we have seen, the emergence of the Great Society fundamentally altered reality for citizens in the United States of America and beyond. This process had been set in motion by the industrial and technological revolutions, which had been driven by modern science and ushered in modernity. Dewey highlighted the fact that whilst the physical forces of the industrial-technological revolutions had 'revolutionised the face of the globe', the political and moral 'ideas and ideals that rule us are still largely those of a pre-scientific, pre-industrial, pre-technological age'. With this in mind, Dewey declared that it was understandable, even if one could not sympathize with such views, why reactionary and conservative ideologies clamoured for a return to 'simpler conditions'. These viewpoints resorted to a 'mixture of exhortation and with reliance upon traditions, habits, institutions, which were adjusted to bygone conditions'. And although they clamoured for the impossible – a return to political isolation – the rise of fascism, Nazism and state totalitarianism was 'no accident' but the logical conclusion of a disjunction between our political ideals and the reality of the Great Society (LW17: 454, 459).

The problem of the Great Society and its politics, Dewey contended, was that monolithic theories and ideologies of social action tended to have 'ready-made' answers to a context that was prone to changing and which demanded new solutions. However, if Dewey (LW1: 358) was adamant that the 'industrial-technological revolution was largely, if not wholly, responsible for the two world wars and the threat of another of ultimate destructiveness', he was also adamant about the 'potential alliance between scientific and democratic method and the need of consummating this potentiality' in tackling the problems and publics generated by the Great Society (LW13: 135). Moreover, Dewey believed that the 'crisis in democracy' demanded the 'substitution of intelligence that is exemplified in scientific procedure for the kind of intelligence that is now accepted' (LW11: 51). This alliance between the scientific and the democratic method is what Dewey calls 'social intelligence'.

To understand Dewey's idea of social intelligence, we must first recall Dewey's ideas of creative democracy and democratic community that we explored in Chapter 1. Creative democracy points towards the perpetual adaption of social institutions, including democratic institutions and practices themselves, as new publics are engendered by social change. This is founded on the ethical commitment of democracy as a way of life to the principle that those who are affected by social institutions should have an equality of opportunity to contribute to the production and management of those institutions. The balanced equality of democracy as a way of life and its focus on collective problem-solving highlights Dewey's faith in a deliberative (conference, consultation, negotiation and persuasion) form of political settlement and the establishment of a democratic community.

What, then, is the role of social intelligence in creative democracy and in the maintenance of the democratic community? The answer centres on the form of deliberation within the democratic community. Dewey cautioned that public discussion and comparison of ideas alone were inherently too weak to meet the problems brought about by the movements of the Great Society (LW11: 50–2).[3] Social intelligence is thus not simply the practice of democratic deliberation, but rather a certain way of democratically practising deliberation. Quintessentially, social intelligence attempts to adapt the 'experimental method' of natural science in the arena of human relations. This does not mean that particular techniques of natural science were to be simply transposed into social contexts or that laboratory experimentation was to be carried out on society at large. Whilst Dewey did not discount the use of such scientific methods in social affairs, he primarily saw the key part of social intelligence as centring on the transposition of the 'attitude of the mind exemplified in the conquest of nature by experimental science' into 'social affairs' (LW9: 108). Social intelligence therefore attempts to utilize elements of natural science's 'attitude of the mind' to promote an array of habits, a personal way of living, which perpetuates democracy as a way of life in the day-to-day lives of citizens (LW7: 329–30).

In the first instance, Dewey outlines that social intelligence would see individuals possess 'democratic habits of thought and action', which stem from the scientific attitude of the mind, and that they would practise such methods in 'all social relationships' (LW11: 225). Dewey outlines this 'distinctive type of disposition and purpose' as habits of thought and action that would promote:

> ...willingness to hold beliefs in suspense, ability to doubt until evidence is obtained; willingness to go where evidence points instead of putting first a personally preferred conclusion; ability to hold ideas in solution and use them as hypotheses to be tested instead of dogmas to be asserted; and (possibly the most distinctive of all) enjoyment of new fields for enquiry and of new problems. (LW13: 166)

Through such habits, Dewey contends, members of a society can substitute the utilization of unquestioned moral truths, such as class interests, pride and prejudice, commands of the state, constitutions or traditions, with a process of social intelligence that utilizes the 'experimental method' of forming social policy and morality as 'co-operative undertakings' between members of a community (LW7: 329; LW14: 228).

The term 'experimental method' may erroneously suggest Dewey's embracement of moral relativism or the belief that all past moral precedents that provide the basis for established social policy are to be lightly discarded. However, the overriding point of the adoption of the scientific attitude to the appraisal of moral conflict is the belief that there can be no assumption of an a priori truth that would automatically adjudicate moral conflict or provide the basis for social policy. Eschewing moral relativism, the experimental method places its faith in demonstrable evidence rather than dogmatic moral absolutes when appraising moral conflict and the merits of social policy. In the light of this, an experimental method of forming social policy and morality is simply how members of a society, who share a common embracement of the scientific attitude, collectively appraise moral conflict and the merits of respective social policy. Dewey defines the experimental method as a 'reflective morality' that:

> ... demands observation of particular situations, rather than fixed adherence to *a priori* principles; that free enquiry and freedom of publication and discussion must be encouraged and not merely grudgingly tolerated; that opportunity at different times and places must given for trying different measures so that their effects maybe be capable of observation and of comparison with one another. (LW7: 329)

In this scenario, the machinations of the cultural matrix and social policy are to be approached in terms of an analysis of cause and effect and means and consequences (LW11: 52). Just as past principles, precedents or points of authority are used in natural science, social policies are to be used as 'working hypotheses' which, based on the knowledge of past experience, act as tools that help us manage material culture towards desired ends. Established social policies are to be no more easily discarded than established scientific principles but they are to be continually subject to 'constant' and 'well-equipped' inquiry, observation and reflection upon the consequences they entail. Dewey dubs such an approach 'experimental', however, because on the back of such observation and reflection, which may bring to light newly discovered evidence or conditions within the cultural matrix that lead to doubt over their soundness or acceptability, all social policies and the moral values which engender them are to be open to revision or alteration (LW7: 329–30).[4]

Social intelligence therefore mandates that deliberation within the democratic community is not to be a fight over notions of antecedent and independent conceptions of morality or social policy but rather the experimental formation of moral value and social policy in response to evidence. The underlying premise of this process is that 'day-to-day working together with others' is the best solution to social problems. As Kloppenburg (1994: 79) contends, Dewey's idea of the democratic community and the use of social intelligence replicate what Dewey saw as the chief tenets of the scientific community:

> No scientific inquirer can keep what he finds to himself or turn it to merely private account without losing his scientific standing. Everything discovered belongs to the community of workers. Every new idea and theory has to be submitted to this community for confirmation and test. There is an expanding community of cooperative effort and of truth. (LW5: 115)

Under the remit of social intelligence, differing or conflicting moral parties do not merely deliberate their positions but actually explore their conflict as a problem to be solved by embracing the scientific attitude and the experimental method of forming social policy and morality. This means not only having the willingness to learn from the moral positions and evidence about the machinations of society and associated behaviour put forward by different publics, but also having the willingness to surrender such a conflict to constant and well-equipped inquiry and observation, and then for both sides to co-operate in solving such moral conflict:

> .... even when needs and ends or consequences are different for each individual, the habit of amicable cooperation – which may include, as in sport, rivalry and competition – is itself a priceless addition to life. To take as far as possible every conflict which arises – and they are bound to arise – out of the atmosphere and medium of force, of violence as a means of settlement into that of discussion and of intelligence is to treat those who disagree – even profoundly – with us as those from who we may learn, and in so far, as friends… To cooperate by giving difference a chance to show themselves because of the belief that the expression of difference is not only a right of the other persons but is a means of enriching one's own life experience, is inherent in the democratic personal way of life. (LW14: 228)

Dewey's idea of creative democracy must therefore be seen as an evolutionary form of democracy predicated upon the widespread use of social intelligence in the appraisal of moral conflict over social policy. It was the maintenance of the democratic community through the methods of social intelligence, Dewey believed, which would allow moral conflicts and the resultant social policy decisions to be settled in the 'widest possible contribution of all – or at least the great majority' (LW11: 56).

The obvious question that follows from this discussion is this: Why did Dewey believe social intelligence to be the best method for approaching moral and political conflict? Dewey believed that social intelligence, whilst not a panacea for all social problems, held the greatest hope of bringing 'order and even abundance to societies plagued by strife and uncertainty' (Gouinlock 1990: 268). In the first instance, this was based on the non-absolutism of social intelligence allowing for all moral positions to be voiced, heard and evaluated through social intelligence. In this sense, social intelligence provided publics with the best method of voicing grievances and a collaborative process of political settlement that avoided the recourse to violence and coercive control:

> When democracy openly recognizes the existence of *problems* and the need for probing them *as* problems as its glory, it will relegate political

groups that pride themselves upon refusing to admit incompatible opinions to the obscurity which already is the fate of similar groups in science. (LW13: 135)

Dewey pushed this position even further by suggesting that 'social control effected through organised application of social intelligence' was the only form of political settlement that could deal with 'existing evils without landing us firmly in some form of coercive control from above and outside' (LW 13: 320).

Dewey's faith in a form of creative democracy through social intelligence was also based on what he saw as the productive gains the scientific community had bequeathed to humanity and the possible gains it could provide for humanity within the sphere of moral and political matters. This process within science seemingly validated the co-operative inquiry of social intelligence:

> The contrast between the state of intelligence in politics and in the physical control of nature is to be taken literally. What has happened in this latter is the outstanding demonstration of the meaning of organized intelligence. The combined effect of science and technology has released more productive energies in a bare hundred years than stands to the credit of prior human history in its entirety... The stationary engine, the locomotive, the dynamo, the motorcar, turbine, telegraph, telephone, radio and moving picture are not the products of either isolated individual minds nor of the particular economic régime called capitalism. They are the fruit of methods that first penetrated to the working causalities of nature and then utilized the resulting knowledge in bold imaginative ventures of invention and construction. (LW11: 52)

Dewey located the revolutions of science that in turn led to the industrial-technological revolutions as revealing the social nature of intelligence. In this regard, science highlighted how intelligence was a 'social asset' with a public origin based on social co-operation (LW11: 48). Moreover, science and its sense of community highlighted to Dewey that allowing individuals to share in the fruits of community would allow the effective intelligence of all to rise considerably. Indeed, Dewey stated that in 'a social medium in whose institutions the available knowledge, ideas and art of humanity were incarnate the average individual would rise to undreamed of heights of social and political intelligence' (LW11: 50). Beyond this, however, science also highlighted how the social nature of intelligence could lead to unthinkable advancements across society when teamed with the experimental method of approaching problems through the co-operative undertakings. Dewey's hope was that the democratic community could realize the method of the scientific community through using social intelligence, and in doing so, correct the failure to utilize 'human power' in the same way science had utilized nature to realize productive energies:

> The general adoption of the scientific attitude in human affairs would mean nothing less than a revolutionary change in morals, religion, politics and industry. The fact we have limited its use so largely to technical matters is not a reproach to science, but to the human beings who use it for private ends and who strive to defeat its social application for fear of destructive effects upon their power and profit. A vision of a day in which the natural science and the technologies that flow from them are used as servants of a humane life constitutes the imagination that is relevant to our own time. (LW5: 115)

This may all sound like wishful thinking and Dewey was willing to admit that he himself may be exaggerating the power of co-operation vis-à-vis ideas of class conflict or the inherent evil within humanity. But in the context of the greatest crisis of liberal democracy and the rise of totalitarianisms, Dewey contended that social intelligence was 'worth a trial' and that 'illusion for illusion', this particular one may be better 'than those humanity has usually depended upon' (LW9: 108). More to the point, Dewey was adamant that a society and culture that permitted science to destroy traditional values but which distrusted its power to create new ones was a culture which was 'destroying itself' (LW13: 172).[5]

The planning society

Dewey believed that social intelligence highlighted that humans were capable of 'intelligent' judgement and action, both individually and collectively, when appraising social problems and forming social policy (creative democracy), if equipped with an equality of communication and participation in democratic life (democracy as a way of life), the right intellectual sensibility and habits (scientific attitude) and the free play of facts and ideas (experimental method). This was the co-joining of the democratic method with the scientific method. However, Dewey was certainly no believer that bourgeois democracy was hospitable to such a method or that citizens widely possessed democratic habits of social intelligence. As we encountered in Chapter 3, Dewey's take on bourgeois democracy and its pernicious effects on the 'intelligence' of the masses are quite clear. The hegemony of finance capitalism and its creation of vast material and cultural inequality stunted any chance of creative democracy through limiting both the participation and intelligence of the masses. This not only neglected the ethical commitment of the democratic as a way of life but also failed to utilize them as a resource for the practice of social intelligence. As Dewey outlines, bourgeois democracy gave no opportunity for the great mass of people:

> ... to reflect and decide upon what is good for them. Others who are supposed to be wiser and who in any case have more power decide the question for them and also decide the methods and means by which subjects may arrive at the enjoyment of what is good for them. This form of coercion and suppression is more subtle and more effective than is overt intimidation and restraint. When it is habitual and embodied in social institutions, it seems the normal and natural state of affairs. The mass usually become unaware that they have a claim to a development of their own powers. Their experience is so restricted that they are not conscious of restriction. It is part of the democratic conception that they as individuals are not the only sufferers, but that the whole social body is deprived of the potential resources that should be at its service. (LW11: 218–19)

Dewey argued that the 'ultimate' institution, which could help mitigate the lack of democratic habits amongst the masses, was education and educational reform. Education 'more than other single agency, is concerned with the development of free inquiry, discussion and expression' (LW11: 253). However, Dewey did not believe that bourgeois democracy and the results it generated could be patched up 'here and there' through sporadic reforms to areas such as education. Instead, what was first and foremost needed was the recognition of the 'moral, emotional and intellectual effect' the day-to-day workings of the political economy of bourgeois democracy had upon all citizens:

> ... every one who reflects upon the subject admits that it is impossible that the ways in which activities are carried on for the greater part of the waking hours of the day; and the way in which the shares of the individuals are involved in the management of affairs in such a matter as gaining a livelihood and attaining material and social security, can only be a highly important factor in shaping personal dispositions; in short, forming character and intelligence. (LW11: 221)

In order to facilitate the spread of democratic habits of social intelligence amongst the masses, it was imperative, Dewey argued, that the 'profit system' of capitalism be reoriented to one which would realize that the 'ultimate problem of production is the production of human beings' (LW13: 318). To accomplish this, Dewey put forward the idea of reorientating the American economy around a form of democratic socialism. This centred on adopting various ideas from the 'British Labour Party and Social Democratic Parties of Europe' and required the socialization of the 'commanding heights of the economy' through creating publics works, enacting taxes that could deliver a thorough redistribution of wealth and the nationalization of industries (LW9: 289–90). However, Dewey envisioned a socialized economy that was not simply a form of state socialism. A socialized economy was to provide the platform that would facilitate creative democracy through the practice of social intelligence. This move for economic freedom was thus geared towards securing the cultural freedom needed to perpetuate social intelligence (LW11: 254). This included the aforementioned reforms to education, the media and the arts, but also an increased workplace democracy and a remodeling of the state and its political democracy towards resolving moral conflicts between publics (Westbrook 1991: 457).

The twining of a socialized economy with participatory democracy provided the grounds for what Dewey saw as the difference between the 'planning society' of democratic socialism vis-à-vis the 'planned society' of bourgeois democracy and its communist and fascist alternatives. A planning society was essentially another name for what Dewey believed would be the practices of creative democracy in the Great Community. Such a society would not just drift from problem to problem but actively use social intelligence in order to practise creative democracy and perpetuate the future use of social intelligence through a diffusion of democratic habits across society:

> What *claims* to be social planning is now found in Communist and Fascist countries. The *social* consequence is complete suppression of freedom of inquiry, communication and voluntary association, by means of a combination of personal violence, culminating in the extirpation, and systematic partisan propaganda. The results are such that in the minds of many persons the very idea of social planning and of the violation of the integrity of the individual are becoming intimately bound together. But an immense difference divides the *planned* society from a *continuously planning* society. The former requires fixed blueprints imposed from above and therefore involving reliance upon physical and psychological force to secure conformity to them. The latter means the release of intelligence through the widest form of cooperative give-and-take. The attempt to *plan* social organization and association without the freest possible play of intelligence contradicts the very idea of *social planning*. For the latter is an operative method of activity, not a predetermined set of final truths.
> (LW13: 321)

Dewey's faith in the democratic planning can be found not only in his philosophical work but also in his political activism during the Great Depression and the New Deal era. Many of his statements on democratic socialism come from publications and activism linked to the People's Lobby (PL) and the League for Independent Political Action (LIPA). Even critics of Dewey's social theory point to the fact that groups such as the PL, LIPA and the Farmer-Labour Political Federation (FLPF) provided the politics that Dewey's '...ideals and his political theory demanded'. These were organizations that showed Dewey's belief that the two dominant political parties of the United States were under the spell of bourgeois democracy and were unable and unwilling to stand up to the power of capital. These groups therefore campaigned to create new forms of alliance between agricultural farmers, the working class and the middle class in the pursuit and hope of founding a new third political party. Moreover, Dewey's pursuit of radical 'third party' politics within the United States sought to create the very organizations that could help educate and inform the eclipsed public he had talked about since the 1920s, and also sought to 'invest them with the power to define their interests and reconstruct the state' (Westbrook 1991: 452).

Democracy and equality

The details of Dewey's democratic socialism have always stoked debate amongst Deweyan scholars and interlocutors. In the essay the 'End of Leninism', Richard Rorty, perhaps Dewey's most infamous philosophical interpreter of the twentieth century, states that Dewey was calling for nothing short of the wide-scale replacement of the market economy. Rorty goes on to argue that such thought, in the light of the latter half of the twentieth century and the fall of organized communism, was simply outdated and proven to be a political and moral dead end (Rorty 1998: 329n15). On the other hand, Robert Westbrook (2005: 171) – Dewey's most famous historical interpreter – believes Rorty's own interpretation went too far and concealed the fact that Dewey's vision of democratic socialism was of a 'semi-socialist' market economy regulated in the interests of the least well off. It is beyond the remit of this book to settle the debate about the details of Dewey's vision of the democratic socialism and its political economy.[6] However, we can make the argument as to why Dewey sought to achieve democratic socialism in the first place. At the heart of Dewey's vision of political economy were ideas about the need to secure economic equality to ensure the ethical commitment of democracy as a way of life and the diffusion of democratic habits that would facilitate social intelligence. This was because the Great Society had unleashed forces which, when interpreted through the lens of bourgeois democracy and its ideas of liberty, could perpetually undermine the democratic way of life and the use of social intelligence.

Dewey's ideas about the relationship between economic and political equality can be gleaned from his critique of the New Deal. Castigating it as an inadequate 'half-way house' between unregulated capitalism and democratic socialism, Dewey saw that the New Deal as ideological enterprise designed 'to save the profit system from itself' (LW9: 289). The reforms of Roosevelt, Dewey argued, were nothing more than temporary measures which as 'sure as night follows day' would inevitability lead back to restoring the power and privilege of bourgeois democracy (LW9: 77). By 1939, Dewey was even more adamant that the 'profit' system of capitalism was incapable of democratic ends:

> The means have to be implemented by a social-economic system that establishes and uses the means for the production of free human beings associating with one another on terms of equality. Then and then only will these means be an integral part of the end, not frustrated and self-defeating, bringing new evils and generating new problems. (LW13: 320)

The question then becomes why did Dewey believe that the social-economic system he encountered was incapable of producing free human beings associating with one another on terms of equality? And how did this result in Dewey arguing for democratic socialism within the confines of the Great Society?

The answers to these questions are best illustrated in Dewey's reconstruction of liberalism and liberty in *Liberalism and Social Action* (LW11) and a whole swathe of essays written throughout the

Great Depression. In these works, Dewey puts forward the idea that 'liberalism' and its idea of liberty had become a much-confused concept and departed from its initial meaning (LW11: 5). If we recall the discussion of philosophical liberalism in Chapter 3, Dewey highlighted that the advent of bourgeois democracy had seen the ideas of liberty, individualism and democracy become fused with the ideal of laissez-faire capitalism (LW11: 250). Dewey, however, took this conception of liberty and individualism to task. Outlining the fact that liberty is not a static or general concept, Dewey contends that liberty is best conceived as 'power, the effective power to do specific things'. This demand for power was always historically located and based on the distribution of power that 'exists at the time'. The system of liberties is always just a 'system of restraints or controls that exists at that time'. As a result, Dewey argued that there was no such thing as 'liberty or effective power of an individual group, or class' except in relation to the 'liberties, the effective powers, of other individuals, groups and classes'. This revealed the social nature of liberty, where 'the liberties that any individual actually has depended upon the distribution of powers and liberties' engendered by the legal, political and economic structures of society (LW11: 361–2).

Dewey argued that when liberty was rightfully taken as a historically relative concept, philosophical liberalism's rendering of 'liberty', 'individualism' and 'democracy' as historically chained to ideas of laissez-faire capitalism was simply a denial of the historical relativity of liberty. More to the point, such an ahistorical idea of liberty concealed the fact that ideas that once espoused freedom, bringing about the 'glorious revolution' of 1688 and eighteenth- and nineteenth-century democratic revolts against oligarchical government, had become a form of 'pseudo-liberalism' that ossified an illiberal form of social organization (LW11: 287, 291). The ideas of liberty, individualism and democracy that were tied to laissez-faire capitalism were now undeniably unfit for purpose and stood against the very ideas they were supposed to represent:

> ... *laissez-faire* liberalism is played out, largely because of the fruits of its own policies. Any system that cannot provide elementary security

for millions has no claim to the title of being organized in behalf of the liberty and the development of individuals. (LW11: 287)

Dewey was adamant that the entire meaning of liberalism and liberty must now be reconstructed to help facilitate creative democracy and the habits of social intelligence in the midst of the Great Society. To this end, Dewey recovered what he called the 'formula of early democratic political liberalism' that located the relationship between equality and liberty and recognized the historical relativity associated with obtaining this goal. This conception of democratic liberty, which in the hands of Dewey was another name for the democratic way of life, viewed that all humans are and were 'born free and equal'. This was not a foolish belief in the equality of individual endowments but rather the belief that political equality was the product of social institutions, laws, and customs and habits. Within this idea of liberty, social institutions and laws should always act 'as such to secure and establish equality for all' in order to perpetuate the democratic ideal. This recovering of the 'formula of early democratic political liberalism' revealed that equality, liberty and fraternity were not incompatible but rather that the 'actual liberties of one human being depend upon the powers of action that existing institutional arrangements accord to other individuals' (LW11: 369–70). To secure its ethical commitment, the democratic way of life therefore always demanded a historically relative democratic distribution of liberties (Westbrook 1991: 436).

When Dewey utilized this 'formula of early democratic political liberalism', it became clear to him that an economic reorganization of the Great Society must be at the centre of a democratic distribution of liberties. Whilst Dewey did not discount the importance of economic relations across history, the context of the Great Society now meant that industry, banking and commerce had reached a point where 'private business enterprise' affected so many people in 'deep and enduring ways' that all 'business' was held a potential 'public interest'. Since the 'consequences of business' were now social, society must itself look after 'the industrial and financial causes of these consequences' (LW11: 287). This in turn formed the rationale of Dewey's ideas that a reconstructed liberalism would have to centre on a form of democratic socialism in order to live up to the democratic way of life because the social consequences of laissez-faire liberalism, namely its cultural and economic inequality, now prevented liberty for all:

> ...the ends which liberalism has always professed can be attained only as control of the means of production and distribution is taken out of the hands of individuals who exercise powers created socially for narrow individual interests. The ends remain valid. But the means of attaining them demand a radical change in economic institutions and the political arrangements based upon them. These changes are necessary in order that social control of forces and agencies socially created may accrue to the liberation of all individuals associated together in the great undertaking of building a life that expresses and promotes human liberty. (LW11: 367)

What is pivotal to note here, however, is that Dewey's reconstructed liberalism along democratic socialist lines makes a distinct statement about the role of economic equality in the maintenance of the democratic way of life and the possibility of social intelligence within the context of the Great Society. The industrial-technological revolutions of the Great Society and their control by 'finance-capitalism' through the ideology of laissez-faire liberalism had given liberty of action to certain citizens and groups with '...abilities of acquiring property and to the employment of that wealth in further acquisitions'. The favouring of such abilities not only created an insidious link between capital and industry and science, but also saw the creation of economic inequalities that impoverished political democracy and secured the 'monopoly of power in the hands of the few to control the opportunities of the wide masses and to limit their free activities in realizing their natural capacities' (LW11: 369–70). Dewey stressed that this meant that a democratic distribution of liberties was now only possible through the establishment of economic equality:

> The democratic ideal that unites equality and liberty is, on the other hand, recognition that actual and concrete liberty of opportunity and action is dependant upon equalization of the political and economic

> conditions under which individuals are alone free *in fact*, not *in some abstract metaphysical way*. The tragic breakdown of democracy is due to the fact that the identification of liberty with the maximum of unrestrained individualistic action in the economic sphere, under the institutions of capitalistic finance, is as fatal to the realization of liberty for all as it is fatal to the realization of equality. It is destructive of liberty for the many precisely because it is destructive of genuine equality of opportunity. (LW11: 370)

This was because the genie of the industrial-technological revolutions and the ideas of laissez-faire liberalism could not simply be put back in the lamp. It was inevitable, Dewey argued, that if such ideas and practices were left unchecked and remained hegemonic that they would seize the fruits of industrial-technological revolutions and generate a form of economic inequality that would perpetually nullify any chance of creative democracy:

> The drift of nominal democracy from the conception of life which may properly be characterized as democratic has come about under the influence of a so-called rugged individualism that defines the liberty of individuals in terms of the inequality bred by existing economic-legal institutions. In so doing, it puts almost exclusive emphasis upon those natural capacities of individuals that have power to effect pecuniary and materialistic acquisitions. For our existing materialism, with the blight to which it subjects the cultural development of individuals, is the inevitable product of the exaggeration of the economic liberty of the few at the expense of the all-around liberty of the many. And, I repeat, this limitation upon genuine liberty is the inevitable product of the inequality that arises and must arise under the operations of institutionally established and supported finance-capitalism. (LW11: 371)[7]

If one took liberty to mean the 'power to act' and a democratic conception of liberty to mean the 'power to act equally', then it became clear to Dewey that only an equal distribution of power within economic circles would now facilitate genuine political equality within the context of the Great Society. Dewey thus declared that the 'future of democracy' within the context of cultural matrix of the Great Society now centred on how democracy could be made secure in a context where most people have the 'minimum' of control over the conditions of their own subsistence. The democratic way of life would now have to be twined with the idea of using 'political action to bring about equalisation of economic conditions in order that the equal right of all to free choice and free action be maintained' (LW13: 178, 300). When this is taken into consideration, Dewey's arguments for democratic socialism read as nothing more as the means to achieve a democratic distribution of liberty (power) within the Great Society:

> Power today resides in control of the means of production, exchange, publicity, transportation and communication. Whoever owns them rules the life of the country, not necessarily by intention, not necessarily by deliberate corruption of the nominal government, but by necessity. Power is power and must act, and it must act according to the nature of the machinery through which it operates. In this case, the machinery is business for private profit through private control of banking, land, industry, reinforced by command of the press, press agents and other means of publicity and propaganda. In order to restore democracy, one thing and one thing only is essential. The people will rule when they have power, and they will have power in the degree they own and control the land, the banks, the producing and distributing agencies of the nation. Ravings about Bolshevism, Communism, Socialism are irrelevant to the axiomatic truth of this statement. They come either from complaisant ignorance or from the deliberate desire of those in possession, power and rule to perpetuate their privilege. (LW9: 76–77)

Whatever the debate about the details of Dewey's democratic socialism and its political economy, it becomes apparent that Dewey believed that economic security and equality for the masses would have to be secured in order for democracy as a way of life to live up to its own ethical commitment within the context of the Great Society. Unlike Marxist positions, which posited a metaphysical argument about alienation to call for a wholesale change of the economic system (LW13: 116–35), Dewey did not turn to democratic socialism because he believed it would reconcile man with himself but because he saw such ideas and practices as the best means to achieving a democratic distribution of liberties in the midst of the industrial-technological revolutions of the Great Society and laissez-faire liberalism. Moreover, this move towards securing 'greater measures of economic freedom for the mass of people' was not an end in itself but rather was the means to secure political equality and the 'means' within the Great Society to secure the 'cultural freedom' which would facilitate the emergence of the Great Community and allow the human '... development through science, art and unconstrained human intercourse' (LW11: 254). This cultural freedom was about securing the diffusion of habits that would help facilitate the use of social intelligence. However, the chief point here is that Dewey put forward a historically rooted argument that such cultural freedom was now only possible through mutually reinforcing forms of equality of political opportunity and equality of economic outcome.[8]

Global democracy and equality

The obvious question that arises from the discussion of Dewey's idea about the relationship between economic equality and democracy in the Great Society surrounds its global connotations. After all, the Great Society was shorthand not simply for American corporate capitalism but also for the complex global capitalist economy that was initiated by the long nineteenth century and the First Great Globalization. Would Dewey's work then lend itself towards a global democratic distribution of liberties and a global equalization of economic conditions? Moreover, can Dewey's work on democracy and equality offer us a form of global justice?

This question has most recently been approached by Phillip Deen (2013), who has attempted to see if philosophical pragmatism and, in particular, Dewey's work can offer an account of global distributive justice. Taking the process of social intelligence and its use to solve moral problems as the essential commitment of philosophical pragmatism,

Deen outlines that for writers such as Dewey 'a just global order is one that provides the conditions for fruitful democratic inquiry on matters crossing boundaries, both physical and conceptual, between states or peoples'. Moreover, Deen contends that pragmatism, and in particular Dewey's work, develops two ends of a continuum between the ideal and non-ideal conditions for producing a just international order (Deen 213: 112–16). These two ends are:

1. A just order that addresses concrete problems at the international level – such as global climate change, gross economic inequality between nations and human rights – that utilizes the social intelligence and its experimental method to form moral value and social policy between nation states and publics within and between nation states. The use of ideal models here would be to test 'experimentally' in order to show how they can solve global problems.
2. Certain practical conditions must be brought about to ensure that social intelligence can take place. These include institutional arrangements, such as rights of expression and freedom of information and assembly, that facilitate social intelligence and lessening of the distorted effects of poverty and inequality.

Deen goes on to argue that 'long experience' has determined the 'necessary conditions' for social intelligence and allows us to assert that 'relatively stable ends for inquiry' require us to now 'free people from great want, oppression or ignorance' (Deen 2013: 116).[9] Deen prefigures his paper with two disclaimers. One is that his work does not take into account historical development of Dewey's writings on international politics. The second is that his work is 'unabashedly speculative' (Deen 2013: 112). In response to this, we can say that Deen's work need not be speculative as creative democracy through social intelligence was what Dewey wished to come to pass both at home and aboard. As Dewey stated in 1944:

> Just as genuinely peaceful relations amongst nations cannot be secured save by systematic intelligent study, foresight and planning, so with

democracy within a nation. The development of procedures and techniques, legal, political, economic, which will foster and sustain equal freedom for all, instead of irresponsible freedom for a few and constraint and depression for the many, is the outstanding social problem of our age. It requires the kind of vigilance which is positively expressed in study, planning, experimentation, to establish institutions which will make equality of opportunity and hence freedom realities for all – not slogans to be manipulated by a class for its one separate interest. (LW17: 462)

Moreover, had Deen examined Dewey's work on international politics and the need for creative democracy at the international level, he would have found arguments that both support and extend beyond his own ideas. Dewey believed that the ethical commitment of democracy as a way of life and social intelligence must be supported at the international level. However, Dewey did not just throw his weight behind a regime that would secure a global minimalism that would only free people from great want, oppression or ignorance. Rather, Dewey extended his arguments about equality and democracy within the confines of bourgeois democracy at home into the international arena of the Great Society.

As Dewey outlined, the ideas of philosophical liberalism about equality and liberty seemed even more hegemonic at the international level. This regime of 'free-trade' was 'hopelessly defective' because it failed to see how 'intelligent supervision' and 'positively controlling action' were needed to maintain 'equality of conditions' (MW11: 141). This state of affairs had led to a game of 'rivalry and competition in industry and nationalistic ambitions' that had 'extended to become a deadly competition in all the means of destruction' (LW17: 454). Nations and their publics now routinely neglected the social aspects of their interdependence and saw global interdependence as a zero-sum game:

> Bad results work both ways. In order to compete with other nations, a competition artificially made harder by the present system of barriers, labour standards are lowered at home. Then other nations find that

unless wages are reduced at home and labour speeded up, they are at a disadvantage. Their standards are put in peril. We have made almost universal the inquiry of Cain: "Am I my brother's keeper?" We have erected indifference and antagonism into a positive virtue, although we know in domestic affairs that depression of one group and section, means loss to all others. (LW11: 262)

As early as Dewey's post–First World War writings, one can glean a sense of disdain for such liberal ideas about international free trade and the global economy and how such ideas expressed themselves through imperialism, asymmetric North/South relations and large-scale inequalities. As Dewey outlined in 1918 on the subject of President Wilson's new diplomacy, the League of Nations and economic freedom, these material inequalities ultimately prohibited the extension of democracy as a way of life at the international level:

> It has been demonstrated that more is needed to secure freedom and equality of conditions between individuals than to declare them legally all free and equal, while leaving them to unrestricted competition with one another. Immense inequality of power is compatible with formal equality. The same thing will surely develop with respect to any merely legal equality among nations. Certain nations have a tremendous superiority in population, natural resources, technical progress in industry, command of credit, and shipping. Nothing better calculated to develop inequality of trade relationship among nations could well be found than a system which set up a nominal mathematical equality and then threw matters practically into the hands of the present big nations. (MW 11: 139)

Dewey's idea of equality between nations thus did not centre on free trade within a liberal-capitalist global economy but a system of trade and commerce that would eradicate imperialism and inequality in its economic, political and cultural manifestations. This resembled a form of democratic socialism at international level and would require, as Dewey outlined at the end of the First World War, a global economy that was democratically controlled, and international organizations that could deal with matters such as 'equality of labour standards, the regulation of shipping... of food, raw materials and immigrants, and above all else the exportation of capital and distribution of the available credit of the world. Equality of trade conditions means equalisation of conditions' (MW11: 139–40). Global democracy for Dewey would therefore require that rich nations of the world give up their hegemonic control of the global economy and allow the self-government and development of wealth amongst poor nations (Westbrook 1991: 237).[10]

What the above reveals is that Dewey believed that the practice of creative democracy through social intelligence between nations was unlikely to transpire within a global regime based on liberal capitalism. This is quite simply because the global economic regime based on the tenets of liberal capitalism, as it was at home within the nation state, was antithetical towards creating or allowing a context in which such a state of affairs could arise. In short, a liberal-capitalist global economy would always be focused on profit, imperialism and empire rather than democracy as a way of life. To provide the conditions that would allow all members of the world to potentially live the democratic way of life and participate in social intelligence would require furnishing conditions for political equality and of economic development (political, educational, scientific, industrial) that would allow for democratic habits of social intelligence to become widespread both at home and abroad. Thus, Dewey did not believe that transforming the Great Society into the Great Community at international level was simply about managing the economic interdependence of nations or creating equal political standing between nation states. Rather, given the forces of industry the Great Society had unleashed, what was needed was a fundamental reformation of the global liberal-capitalist economy and a form of political and economic equality at the global level. This democratic distribution of liberties in the international arena would allow countries to embark upon pathways that would allow them to acquire and utilize the habits of social intelligence and in turn facilitate the democratic way of life between countries.[11]

Towards the end of the Second World War, Dewey repeated this argument that democracy at the international level also required a democratic distribution of liberties and that to achieve such a distribution of liberties required a fundamental reconfiguration of ideas of equality and liberty and political economy in the international arena:

> The opportunities for us, the people of the United States, will be tremendous. A means for widely distributing the world's goods among all nations must be provided ... A way of carrying health and education and a higher standard of life to the utmost corners of the earth must be assured. The mechanical means have already been produced by science and invention. *Physically*, the world is now one and interdependent. Only human beings – interested that men everywhere have a society of peace, of security, of opportunity, of growth in cooperation – can assure its being made *morally* one. A genuine democratic victory will be achieved only when it is made *by* democratic governments *for* the well-being of the common people of the earth. (LW17: 131–2)

When it comes to issues of global distributive justice, we can say that Dewey was far more radical than critics and supporters are willing to give him credit for. Dewey seems to have been a democratic socialist, both at home and abroad, because the inefficiency of wasting our human resources was not just an American issue but also a global issue. Wasting of such resources not only was a moral problem, which denied various individuals and publics access to the democratic way of life, but was symptomatic of how the Great Society was split between the two worlds of the pre-scientific and the scientific. This not only cost everyone the potential of individual intelligences, who perished each year to the effects of stratification, but such a social order also negatively effected 'effective intelligence' through the cultural subjugation of the great mass of people and denied society and the world at the large the fruits of using socialized intelligence to conduct its moral affairs.

For Dewey, bourgeois democracy and liberal capitalism, both at home and abroad, were thus morally repugnant and physically inefficient; a society which had managed to utilize the natural power of steam, electricity and machines but failed to fully engage, enlist and release available human energy (LW13: 312).[12] The overriding point of this chapter, however, is that Dewey did not believe such problems would be solved without a fundamental reordering of political economy, both at home and abroad, along the lines of economic equality. The gains of the Great Society had quite simply created a situation, where it would be impossible to create the 'enduring opportunity for productive and creative activity and all that signifies for the development of the potentialities of human nature' without 'remaking the profit system' in the first instance (LW13: 318).[13]

5

New Lessons from the Old Professor

The finished and done with is of import as affecting the future, not on its own account: in short, because it is not, really, done with. (MW10: 10)

We do not merely have to repeat the past, or wait for accident to force change upon us. We use our past experiences to construct new and better ones in the future. (MW12: 134)

Dewey's focus on the 'reconstruction' of philosophical and political concepts of democracy was linked, as McDermott (LW11: XXV) argues, to a belief that history was a way of reconstructing the past. The meaning of history was therefore always to be refracted through the perspectives and needs of the present. With that in mind, after journeying through the work of John Dewey and his views on global democracy, it seems that we come to a logical set of questions concerning the relationship between Dewey's time and our own. How are we to use his work for our own purposes? How does Dewey's work help us contemplate and theorize our present form of globalization? And how does Dewey's work inform an analysis of post-Westphalian ideas of global democracy in the twenty-first century?

In the last chapter, I argued against the view that Dewey offered few ideas about how to achieve democracy at home and abroad through examining his views about economic equality. In this chapter, I want to push this line of thought further by outlining what I believe are the solutions Dewey offered to his own problematizing of global democracy and how we can utilize these prescient lessons within our own debates about the nature of global democracy. To highlight this, the chapter will be split into two parts. In the first part, I will outline four key Deweyan lessons about the problem of global democracy. These centre on the nature of society and community, the role of the nation state in furthering democracy beyond the nation state, the use of democracy at home to create a rooted cosmopolitanism and the problem of bourgeois democracy at home as the biggest impediment to global democracy. What all these lessons highlight is how Dewey believed that the problem of democracy at home needed to be tackled in order to facilitate democracy abroad. In the second part, I use these lessons to re-evaluate contemporary ideas about post-Westphalian global democracy and how Dewey's work can offer new ways of appraising global democracy.

Lesson 1: A Great Society does not equal a Great Community

One of the most galling aspects Dewey would have encountered when reading modern ideas about global democracy is how such theorists often conflate the division between society and community and neglect the implications of such a division. From a Deweyan perspective, the first lesson we can learn about global politics is to hold a healthy and historically based scepticism of narratives where our current period of globalization and advancement in modern communications technology or industrial co-operation are said to presuppose the emergence of 'communities of fate', 'transnational public spheres' or any other movement towards a global community. Whilst we may live in a globalized world, it does not automatically mean that our political ideals and identities have also become globalized. Moreover, Dewey provides a historical lesson that such globalized conditions may not necessarily lend themselves to the actual emergence of what he took to be community both on a national and on a global level. For example, Dewey outlines that:

> Associated or joint activity is a condition of the creation of a community. But association itself is physical and organic, while

communal life is moral, that is emotionally, intellectually, consciously sustained. Human beings combine in behaviour as directly and unconsciously as do atoms, stellar masses and cells... They do so in virtue of their own structure, as man and woman unite, as the baby seeks the breast and the breast is there to supply its need. They do so from external circumstances, pressure from without, as atoms combine or separate in presence of an electric charge, or as sheep huddle together from the cold. Associated activity needs no explanation; things are made that way. But no amount of aggregated collective action of itself constitutes a community... Even if "society" were as much an organism as some writers have held, it would not on that account be society. Interactions, transactions, occur *de facto* and the results of interdependence follow. But participation in activities and sharing in results are additive concerns. They demand *communication* as a prerequisite. (LW2: 330)

This distinction between society and community held, for Dewey, not just across local and national societies but also the international associative relationships created by the advent of the Great Society. Although the associative relationships and technological advancements engendered by the Great Society created large-scale global interdependence and industrial co-operation, Dewey did not believe that such conditions alone were sufficient to create, politically and morally, a Great Community. In fact, Dewey believed technological advancements and the accompanying new habits and social customs, engendered by the Great Society's associative relationships, to actually be counterproductive to ideas of community. For instance, we have already seen that Dewey thought that the mass communication revolution (wireless telegraphs, telephones, radio) did not by default create a greater sense of community, or rather the type of communication that generated a sense of community, both within and beyond the nation state. This is even the case when the 'global' context is actively part of our daily discussions:

> We cannot pick up a daily newspaper in which the word "global" does not remind us of the new situation in which we live physically,

but without the intellectual, the educational, the moral preparation that might enable us to cope with the problems it thrusts upon us. (LW17: 454)

Dewey was adamant that a democratic community was enacted through the conscious creation of signs and symbols, habits of thought, language and action and institutions which '... add the function of communication in which emotions and ideas are shared as well as joint undertakings engaged in' (LW13: 176). The emergence and conditions of the Great Society did not automatically lend themselves towards the creation of a Great Community but rather held the potential to facilitate such a goal. In short, the global public or rather global publics will not emerge without conscious action and the conscious dispersion of democratic habits that induce social intelligence both within and beyond the nation state. Dewey therefore provides us with the lesson that democratic communication through habits of social intelligence and the subsequent practice of creative democracy are not things that merely arise from an interdependent society, whether that be across a nation state or the globe, but rather need to be established on the back of the interdependence which arises from societal associations.[1]

Lesson 2: The Great Community and the nation

The discussion of forming a Great Community brings us to the question of the best means of bringing about such a Great Community and the forms of government that would serve it. One of the chief lessons of Dewey's work on the potential for global democracy is that it must include, and also arise within, the nation state. Examining Dewey's account of the Great Society, we can see that his work highlights that the collapse of modern sovereignty is actually a lot older than we care to admit. Throughout the 1920s and 1930s, Dewey continually highlighted how the interdependence of the world's nations had not only seen consequences of associated human action become transnational but also how these transnational consequences affected the ability of nation states to govern properly (LW11: 262). In fact, writing in 1944, Dewey mocked the idea of national sovereignty, arguing that 'something that is wholly unreal in the present state of the world' was being appealed to and employed as if it had 'significance' (LW17: 455). It was on the back of these conditions and outdated policies of nation states that Dewey constructed his own arguments for the extension of democracy globally and took to task what he saw as a bullheaded nationalism which turned 'indifference and antagonism into a positive virtue' in the face of such global interdependence. His subsequent conclusion was that the doctrine of national 'sovereignty', which had buttressed regressive protectionism, quests of autarky and global war, was a complete denial of the political responsibility nation states had towards one another (LW2: 376).

In the light of such statements, one might infer that Dewey would take the national political arena and nationalism to be mere transitory stages in the extension of global democracy. In this sense, the extension of democracy as a way of life would be best served by politically empowering those affected by the consequences of associated action, irrespective of nationality, through cosmopolitan law, global civil society, a transnational public sphere or supranational democratic institutions. After all, as Dewey made clear, political democracy was only effective when the 'government exists to serve its community, and that this purpose cannot be achieved unless the community itself shares in selecting governors and determining their policies' (LW2: 327). Dewey was also under no illusion that the Great Society must become a Great Community that it should be the Great Community that picks its governors.

The problem with this account, however, is whilst Dewey (LW2: 377) recognized the decline of modern sovereignty and his anti-essentialism saw him claim that '*The State* is pure myth', he also understood that the loyalty of citizens to the cultural membership of the nation and its political fusion in the nation state would have to be taken seriously if global democracy was to be successful (LW15: 208–9). Dewey argued that the rise of European nationalism, which was cemented by the

Napoleonic Wars and the resistance to foreign rule, had created a form of nationalism that consolidated 'formerly disperse political and social forces' (LW15: 208). However, this 'modern state unity' had been created not only by resistance to foreign rule but also by the Great Society's technological advancements (railways, telegraph and telephone). These technological advancements in turn created not only the aforementioned economic interdependence amongst the citizens of the nation state, but even more importantly the 'rapid and easy circulation' of opinion and information, which created a national identity beyond the face-to-face communities of people's daily lives and laid the possibility of new forms of national democratic government (LW2: 306–7). This process of cultural membership, contended Dewey, creates a national 'culture' which is exemplified in '...ways of living so ingrained by long habituation that they form the very fibre of a people'. And as the interwar and post–world war periods had made clear, this fibre was so tough 'that it will resist, often unto death, attempts made from without to destroy it' (LW15: 208).[2]

At the start of the twentieth century, then, Dewey recognized what modern writers such as Anderson (1991) and Billig (1995) have pointed out, which is that nation states offer not only legal inclusion but a cultural membership that is always in the process of being remade. Such nationalism, with its exclusive and aggressive side, forms a 'conspicuous' obstacle towards global democracy. However, Dewey also noted that nationalism was 'two-sided' and that the sense of wider social order and organization provided by the nation state and its nationalism should be seen as 'positive advance' (LW15: 208–9). By this, Dewey viewed the nation state as a serious unit of social action not only because of the aggressive side of nationalism but because it was exactly one of those means which have been most expedient in the pursuit of the ethical commitment of democracy as a way of life. The nation state was therefore valuable because it was capable of upholding a national democratic community and a national practice of creative democracy.

With both sides of nationalism in mind, Dewey argued that the nation state and its institutions of democracy could not simply be deemed surplus to requirements or superseded but must play an active part of global democracy:

> A wider community of interests cannot possibly be attained by the negative process of wiping out the communities of belief, action and mutual support which have behind them centuries of loyalty. Without a basis in them, a world government would lead a precarious existence. If such a government is to deserve the hearty support of the peoples of the earth, it must actively enlist the energies of the national states as dependable organs for execution of its politics. It can accomplish this result only as those policies give the social value of the National States a more secure opportunity to flourish than they now possess. (LW15: 209)

Whilst this belief was based on the power of nationalism and national democracy, Dewey also understood the sheer naked power of the nation state. Even within the parameters of declining modern sovereignty, given the role of the nation state in underwriting the structure of the global economy and international institutions, the nation state and, more importantly, national democracy would have to be key focal points of any global democracy. As Dewey's views on the nature of international political economy and political experiments such as the League of Nations highlight, it would simply be impossible to reform the global economy without changing the policies of powerful nation states. The lesson Dewey therefore provides here for twenty-first century observers is that global democracy, which depends on forms of transnational communication and collaboration, equally cannot function on the reification of the global at the expense of the nation state and its politics.[3]

Lesson 3: Democracy begins at home

A Deweyan position mandates that we take the nation state as one of the primary building blocks of any global democracy. The logical consequence of this appraisal of how global democracy could best be enacted is Dewey's subsequent lesson that national conditions of democracy and community are pivotal to forming a Great Community and the practice of global democracy. Moreover, Dewey suggests that without the pursuit of democracy as a way of life and the practice of creative democracy within the local community, there is little chance of the pursuit of democracy as a way of life and practice of creative democracy through social intelligence beyond the nation state:

> It is said, and said truly, that for the world's peace it is necessary that we understand the peoples of foreign lands. How well do we understand, I wonder, our next-door neighbors? It has also been said that if a man love not his fellow man who he has seen, he cannot love the God whom he has not seen. The chances of regard for distant peoples being effective as long as there is no close neighbourhood experience to bring with it insight and understanding of neighbors do not seem better. A man who has not been seen in the daily relations of life may inspire admiration, emulation, servile subjection, fanatical partisanship, hero worship; but not love and understanding, save as they radiate from the attachments of near-by union. Democracy must begin at home, and its home is the neighborly community. (LW2: 368)

The above highlights two interrelated points about the role of the local and national community in the pursuit of global democracy. The first is that the local community, the one of face-to-face intercourse in institutions such as the family, school and neighbourhood, is pivotal in forming other forms of community such as a possible Great Community within the nation state and beyond. This is because it is within these daily and 'face to face' relations that the primary aspects of communication and habits of social intelligence take place. It was therefore within the neighbourly community that the ideals and practice of pursuing a democratic way of life would be taught, learned and put into initial practice. This is why Dewey said that the daily interactions and discourse between members of the local neighbourhood were the 'heart and final guarantee of democracy' (LW14: 227).

The second point is that the local is fundamentally informed and affected by the national and the international dimensions of a globalized world. The Great Society was taken by Dewey to invade and destroy elements of local communities and led to the 'immediate source of the instability, disintegration and restlessness which characterise the present epoch' (LW2: 367). Dewey was adamant that only with the reformation of local community would democracy and community be achievable both within and beyond the state:

> Whatever the future may have in store, one thing is certain. Unless local communal life can be restored, the public cannot adequately resolve its most urgent problem: to find and identify itself. But if it be reestablished, it will manifest a fullness, variety and freedom of possession and enjoyment of meanings and goods unknown in the contiguous associations of the past. For it will be alive and flexible as well as stable, responsive to the complex and world-wide scene in which it is enmeshed. While local, it will not be isolated. Its larger relationships will provide an inexhaustible and flowing fund of meanings upon which to draw, with assurance that its drafts will be honoured... We lie, as Emerson said, in the lap of an immense intelligence. But that intelligence is dormant and its communications are broken, inarticulate and faint until it possesses the local community as its medium. (LW2: 370–2)

What should be noted here is that Dewey was not calling for a nostalgic return to the local democracy that was once characterized by the local 'town-meeting'. Dewey understood that the old ideas of local community town hall meetings that once animated local democracy were now outdated and unable to cope with the engendering of 'national affairs – now also affected by world affairs' (LW13: 95). Whilst Dewey argued for a reconstruction of the local community, this was to be a local community that possessed publics who were adapted to the national and global conditions of the Great Society. The regulation of the Great Society through creative democracy may have depended on a vibrant practice of democratic habits within the local community but Dewey was aware that this could only be facilitated through a national and, in turn, international form of Great Community and creative democracy. Dewey was not a nostalgic advocate of localism but an advocate of a localism now linked to and prepared for the wider world.[4]

This brought Dewey back to the problems of 'home' but this time in the guise of the national community and nation state. The reconstruction of the local community was only possible, Dewey suggested, on the back of a national form of democratic socialism and social intelligence. Furthermore, democracy beyond the state also depended on the vitality of creative democracy within the nation state:

> Our first defence is to realize that democracy can be served only by the slow day by day adoption and contagious diffusion in every phase of our common life of methods that are identical with the ends to be reached and that recourse to monistic, wholesale, absolutist procedures is a betrayal of human freedom no matter in what guise it presents itself. An American democracy can serve the world only as it demonstrates in the conduct of its own life the efficacy of plural, partial and experimental methods in securing and maintaining an ever-increasing release of the powers of human nature, in service of a freedom which is cooperative and a cooperation which is voluntary. (LW13: 187)

Without citizens and publics who can comprehend the complexity and transnational nature of the Great Society and renew democracy as a way of life within the nation state, there is no chance of real political innovation beyond the nation state. The pursuit of global democracy therefore needs publics at home who could not only communicate or organize politically on a transnational basis with other publics, but who could also uphold a form of democratic community and creative democracy at home, which through the use of social intelligence would live up to the ideal of democracy as a way of life both nationally and internationally.

This reveals that Dewey's approach to global democracy was ultimately one of a 'rooted cosmopolitanism' (Bernstein 2010: 88), whereby democracy at home would be key to forging and encouraging democracy abroad. This is an approach where publics approach the global, including transnational activism, in the space of nation states and the resources and opportunities of that national context (Tarrow 2005: 42). This would entail citizens not only creating transnational publics but also seeing their nation state's role in the world not just as a form of moral charity but as a form of political responsibility. This form of political responsibility would include an ethical foreign policy, the use of multilateralism by their leaders to pursue social intelligence between states and an acknowledgement by nation state leaders of transnational publics (Cochran 2001: 56). Above all, however, it would require citizens within nation states to be willing to change their own habits and forms of associative action in order to provide and maintain the democratic way of life for those beyond their borders.[5] As Dewey outlined when commenting on the practice of economic imperialism by US capital and the support of such imperialism by the US state, there was no chance of real political innovation in the relations between the United States and nations it held economic hegemony over without changes in policy and habits within the United States and publics within the United States who could bring such change forward:

> Public opinion has spoken with unusual force and promptitude against interference in Mexico. But the causes of the difficulty, the underlying forces which make for imperialistic ventures, are enduring. They will outlast peaceful escape from the present crisis, supposing we do escape. Public sentiment, to be permanently effective, must do more than protest. It must find expression in a permanent change of our habits. For at present, both economic conditions and political arrangements and traditions combine to make imperialism easy. How many American citizens are ready for an official restatement of the Monroe Doctrine? (LW3: 162)

This view of the need to establish democracy at home in order to help facilitate democracy abroad can also be found in Dewey's thought on the school system in the midst of totalitarianism. Dewey saw the nation's school system as not just a place of training for industry, but also an underutilized arena where there could be a positive and constructive cultivation of the democratic way of life both within and beyond the nation state. Dewey believed that the school, as an institution that taught the democratic way of life, could be reformed and better utilized to '... break down class division, creating a feeling of greater humanity and of a membership in a single family ...' through spreading the habits of social intelligence (LW13: 302). However, Dewey reiterated that he saw this relationship as one where such a global commitment to democracy as a way of life abroad would only be secured through democracy as a way of life at home:

> What do we mean when we assume that we, in common with certain other nations, are really democratic, that we have already so accomplished the ends and purposes of democracy that all we have to do is to stand up and resist the encroachments of non-democratic states? We are unfortunately familiar with the tragic racial intolerance of Germany and now Italy. Are we entirely free from that racial intolerance, so we can pride ourselves upon having achieved a complete democracy? Our treatment of the Negroes, anti-Semitism, the growing (at least I fear it is growing) serious opposition to the alien immigrant within our gates, is, I think, a sufficient answer to that question. Here, in relation to education, we have a problem; what are our schools doing to cultivate not merely passive toleration that will put up with people of different racial birth or different colored skin, but what are our schools doing positively and aggressively and constructively to cultivate understanding and goodwill which are essential to democratic society? (LW13: 301)

Without the realization and practical experience of what 'cooperation, goodwill and mutual understanding' looked like at home, Dewey feared that the ideas of peace that schools were doing a great deal to 'inculcate' would go little beyond 'sentimental attachment to a realisation of what peace would actually mean in the world ...' (LW13: 303). This reflection on education was, in a sense, a microcosm of Dewey's belief that democracy abroad was always linked with democracy at home. It is not just that we cannot examine the chances of global democracy without taking into consideration the status and vitality of our democracy at home, but rather that without a strong form of creative democracy at home, at both the local and national level, there will never be creative democracy away and beyond from home. This is the case even if our ultimate goal is to make the 'away and beyond' our 'home' in the final instance.⁶

Lesson 4: The spectre of bourgeois democracy must be exorcised!

A fuller appreciation of Dewey's work reveals that whilst he embraced multiple routes towards global democracy, he also believed that those routes must include the nation state and the vitality of the local and national community. This point is exemplified in the double mandate Dewey gave his call for democratic renewal within the American nation state. The democratic community within the nation state, Dewey argued, needed to become a Great Community (democratic community) that would help facilitate a Great Community beyond and between nation states. Only through this process would the world secure the democratic way of life for all humans and reap the benefits of social intelligence. However, this brought Dewey back to the problem of bourgeois democracy and the eclipse of the public within the nation state and how bourgeois democracy as an economic, cultural and political formation was fundamentally at odds with creative democracy within and beyond the state.

The main problem that Dewey identified with bourgeois democracy and its influence on global democracy is that the material and cultural inequalities engendered by liberal capitalism are the product of the hegemonic cultural ideas of liberal capitalism (individualism, liberty, profit), which are antithetical to the spread of democratic habits of social intelligence within the nation state. This was confined not only to the level of the nation state but at the international level, where the doctrine of liberal capitalism and free trade between states underpinned a regime of imperialism and inequality between the global North and South. However, Dewey pushes beyond simply equating the culture of liberal capitalism as being incompatible with creative democracy at home and abroad by positing a fundamental relationship between the lack of democracy at home and the lack of democracy abroad.

Moreover, Dewey highlights how the hegemony of the tenets of liberal capitalism and the perpetuation of high levels of material and intellectual inequality within nation states, what Dewey called bourgeois democracy, often bred an anti-cosmopolitan nationalism and the rejection of greater democracy and co-operation at the international level amongst citizens and their governments. This is why Dewey was adamant that it was the eclipse of the public and the breakdown of creative democracy at a national level that explained the lack of global democracy. Dewey therefore extends his narrative of the collapse of community and democracy at the local and national level into the narrative of why the democratic community and creative democracy are absent abroad. The lesson Dewey provides here is that democracy abroad fails due to the same reason democracy at home fails: the eclipse of the public engendered by the cultural and structural inequalities of bourgeois democracy.

Dewey's reflection on the relationship between bourgeois democracy and global democracy therefore outlines his thinking on the relationship between liberal capitalism and democracy. This pivots on Dewey's belief that the ideas and virtues of liberal capitalism are fundamentally unable to support democracy at home or abroad. To this end, the cultural hegemony of the former must be tackled in order to facilitate the emergence of the latter. We have, of course, seen that Dewey was adamant that without the provision of democratic knowledge and habits facilitating social intelligence within social institutions, such as political democracy and education, there was little to no chance of creative democracy at the national level and smaller chance of creative democracy beyond the state. However, Dewey's overriding message was that for the above to happen there must be a fundamental reorganization of liberal capitalism and its ideas of individualism and liberty. This, as we have seen, was Dewey's argument for the extension of a form of democratic socialism and egalitarianism both at home and abroad.[7]

This reflection on the incompatibility of liberal capitalism and democracy and its effects on hopes for democracy beyond the state has knock-on effects on how we should judge Dewey's idea that democracy abroad would only be truly effective on the basis of democracy at home. Dewey's perspective of the nation state as a key vehicle for global democracy translates into the view that we cannot disconnect the current state of national democracy, or a lack of national democracy within bourgeois democracy, from the issues of forming a Great Community and practising creative democracy both within and beyond the state. Although Dewey (LW5: 442) claimed that national democratic practices and institutions had become the 'the errand boys' of a 'privileged plutocracy' and were inflexible and uncreative under the hegemony of bourgeois democracy, it was nevertheless:

> ... sheer defeatism to assume in advance of actual trial that democratic political institutions are incapable either of further development or of constructive social application. Even as they now exist, the forms of representative government are potentially capable of expressing the public will when that assumes anything like unification. (LW11: 60)

The analytical lesson Dewey provides is that the interconnection between the auspices of bourgeois democracy and the possibility of global democracy is exactly why political democracy at home cannot simply be transcended or deemed unimportant when examining global democracy. Quite simply, the issue of who controls the nation state and its institutions and whose interests it serves are too important to the founding of a Great Community and the practice of creative democracy internationally:

> The dominant issue is whether the people of the United States are to control our government, federal, state and municipal, and to use it in behalf of the peace and welfare of society or whether control is to go on passing into the hands of small powerful economic groups who use all the machinery of administration and legislation to serve their own ends. (LW6: 149)

Dewey believed that democratic renewal at home must include a reorganization of both the politics and political economy of bourgeois democracy. This demanded the re-emergence of publics within nation states from their perpetual eclipse in the face of the Great Society and their use of creative democracy through the lens of social intelligence. However, this also demands publics who see that only radical reform of the political economy of bourgeois democracy will facilitate such change (LW11: 298–9).

This reveals Dewey's final lesson on the fate of global democracy in the midst of the Great Society. The renewal of democracy at home demanded the guarantee of the ethical commitment of the democratic way of life and the practising of creative democracy through a community of citizens who possessed the habits of social intelligence. Without such democratic renewal at home and the use of the nation state to pursue a form of rooted cosmopolitanism, it would be impossible, Dewey argued, to achieve the change needed within the international sphere to guarantee the democratic way of life. The chief point, however, is that such a renewal of democracy at home would be half-hearted and unable to secure creative democracy at home or abroad without the political and cultural reorganization of bourgeois democracy at home and the aspiration to effect change in the global liberal-capitalist economy. It was Dewey's hope that America would heed these words and embark upon such a renewal of democracy at home that would provide the conditions for America to help bring about creative democracy abroad:

> With our fortunate position in the world I think that if we used our resources, including our financial resources, to build up among ourselves a genuine, true and effective democratic society, we would find that we have a surer, a more enduring and a more powerful defence of democratic institutions both within ourselves and with relation to the rest of the world than the surrender to the belief in force, violence and war can ever give. (LW13: 302–3)

This should be seen as the final element in Dewey's lessons on the relationship between local and national community and the hopes of forging the Great Society into a Great Community both at home and abroad. Having identified that communities are conscious constructions rather than automatically arising out of societal relations, and that the nation state represented a form of political power and sense of community that could not be easily discarded, Dewey naturally shifted to examining how the politics of the nation and its idea of democratic community could help facilitate democracy beyond the state. This not only required the formation of a democratic community and social intelligence at home but came with a warning that global democracy would be bound to fail without the economic, cultural and political exorcism of the spectres of bourgeois democracy that haunted the Great Society.[8]

Global democracy: A new name for an old problem

John Dewey died in 1952, and his hopes for greater global democracy have remained largely unfulfilled throughout the late twentieth and early twenty-first centuries.[9] However, as prior work on his international thought has shown, it is quite easy to see Dewey as the great resolver of the dualisms that plague the theorizations of global democracy. We can therefore herald Dewey as providing an approach to global democracy that challenges the dualisms between top-down and bottom-up approaches to post-Westphalian global democracy, and between statist and post-Westphalian democracy. Dewey believed in not only macro-reform of international institutions and global governance through a reformation of state relations but also bottom-up processes of publics uniting across the global contours of the Great Society. These ideas not only prefigure an increased role for global governance institutions, such as the UN's responsibility for human security and networks of state special agencies, but also call for an international public sphere of citizens, activists and social movements. Dewey can therefore be seen as an early advocate of the management of international interdependence through the multiple routes of state and non-governmental institutions and practices (Cochran 2010: 323–8).

This take on Dewey's approach to global democracy is superficially correct: the dualisms between top-down and bottom-up ideas of global democracy, and statist and post-Westphalian approaches to global democracy are simply unsustainable. However, this narrative still does not reveal the fullest expression of Dewey's approach to global democracy and how he fundamentally believed the problem of bourgeois democracy at home impacted on democracy abroad. The key lesson of Dewey's work for ideas about global democracy is that whilst a rejection of statist conclusions about global democracy is correct, the importance of the nation state and the status of its democracy and community cannot be discounted within non-statist formulas. Dewey understood that without changes at the national level and in particular its bourgeois democracy, which itself could be helped through transnational communication and collaboration, democracy beyond the state would be hampered and ineffective. Dewey's rooted cosmopolitanism was therefore just that: the strong roots of democracy at home supported the crown of democracy abroad.

This is not the unmasking of Dewey as a proxy statist who dismissed the importance of transnational and non-governmental spaces, such as global civil society and regional or global political forums. As we saw in Chapter 2 and highlighted at the start of this chapter, Dewey can be seen as a thinker who would breach the dualism between state and post-Westphalian positions and between top-down and bottom-up approaches to global democracy. Moreover, his evocation of global civil society reflected his belief that citizens and publics could increase their participation in global democracy through voluntary organizations rather than just investing their hopes of global democracy in national governments or other forms of bureaucracy (Cochran 2010: 327). This would be equally important in the formation and conduct of international institutions, which without the input of the masses of the world would end up as elitist arenas dislocated from the concerns of common humanity. However, Dewey believed that such tactics could only be piecemeal or marginally successful if publics within the nation state did not support such causes and eventually achieve change at the national level.

Dewey would have undoubtedly supported the use of global civil society and transnational forms of activism and communication that use 'boomerang' (Keck and Sikkink 1998) tactics to reach out from local sites to global arenas in order to reverberate back on national policy. Such forms of transnational activism and communication would offer the signs and symbols needed to create elements of community beyond the national context. This today would be what modern writers call transnational coalition formation between publics across borders (Tarrow 2011: 255). This assertion is strengthened by Dewey's own participation in such forms of activism as the Outlawry for War Movement, the Council for a Democratic Germany, the League of Free Nations and the American Friends for Spanish Democracy (Cochran 2010: 310). However, the American base of such activism highlights Dewey's view that without the power of the nation and the vitality of the democratic community, at both the local and national level, there was little chance of democracy beyond the nation state. Dewey's 'rooted cosmopolitanism' therefore reflects the term's modern usage whereby the conduct of global or transnational politics is always domestically rooted (Appiah 1996, 2005: 213–72).

Indeed, contemporary conditions would seem to highlight the continuing saliency and purchase of Dewey's appraisal of global democracy. Writers such as Tarrow (2011: 257) point to fact that 'it has become clear – if it was ever unclear' at the dawn of the twenty-first century, with American military power and government action to tackle the 2008–2009 financial crisis, 'that the power of states is not going to disappear in short order'. Those sceptical of the economic reality of globalization, for example, point to the persistence of nation state power within the confines of neo-liberal globalization and its effects upon modern sovereignty (Mosley 2005; Hay 2007; Hirst et al. 2009). These authors argue that the nature of the flow of trade, investment and finance reveals that the world economy is not global but rather a highly 'internationalized' economy separated into a triad of trade blocs

(Europe, East Asia and North America). Whilst this has changed the nature of global North/South relations, where select nations in the global South have produced miraculous economic growth through exports for consumption zones in the North, the reality is still a highly uneven and unequal global economy largely controlled by and for the global North. This is compounded by the reluctance of hegemonic Western nation states, even in the face of rising Southern powers such as Brazil, China and India, to cede their power within international institutions, such as the UN, IMF and World Bank, and help facilitate greater democracy at the international level (Wade 2013).

In fact, even the runaway world that is neoliberal globalization can be regulated towards democratic ends by nation states. For instance, Hirst et al. (2009) argue that the major economic powers of the G8, China and India have the capacity, if they were to coordinate multilaterally, to bring about greater democratic governance over financial and other international economic practices. However, the current scope of such governance is constrained by the interests of the major economic powers and the hegemony of neo-liberalism amongst political and economic elites (Hirst et al. 2009: 3; Weiss 2009). This viewpoint has gained even more credence in the light of the 2008 financial crisis and the onset of the Great Recession, where the power of the state to intervene in global markets and reform the international order has been shown to outrank international institutions and forums such as the UN, the IMF and the Basel Committee on Banking Supervision (Rodrik 2012). This would seemingly make nation state politics the key for any form of global democracy and is corroborated by the fact that the majority of citizens still predominately value their national identity over other allegiances and see their national governments as the primary providers of public goods (Rodrik 2011; Tarrow 2011).

Concurrently, our present forms of national political democracy are said to be in crisis (Hay 2007). This pivots on the collapse of post-war social democracy and the rise of neo-liberalism, which has engendered large-scale wealth inequality and the hegemony of finance capitalism over the state, its elites and citizens (Stiglitz 2010, 2012; Englen et al.

2011; Wade 2012). This has seen the stagnation of political democracy within the nation state, where national politicians and elites have underwritten globalization and effectively outsourced, renounced or relinquished elements of their political power over to global markets. Concurrently, wealthy citizens whose interests are served by such an ideology find great ease in bending the ear of government to their interests (Gilens 2012). Neo-liberalism's 'atomisation of society, citizens, and classes' has brought forth a mass public who are now 'consumers of goods or information' and have more trust in the Internet than their political representatives (Mazower 2012: 425–6).

Does any of this sound familiar? Our current situation is based upon rich Western nation states who control the global economy and international institutions in their interests; the hegemony of economic liberalism and its idea of economic liberty within international and domestic political contexts; the control of national democratic structures by wealthy citizens and the persistence of large-scale inequality within state; and the continuing pull of nationalism for modern citizens within nation states even in the midst of the breakdown of trust between a large sway of those citizens and their respective governments. Even though there has been so much change since Dewey's death, one could not paint a better picture of the hegemony of liberal capitalism over democracy at the international level and the persistence of bourgeois democracy at home.[10] At the start of the twenty-first century, the regime of liberal capitalism and bourgeois democracy is still partying like it was 1929![11]

With these facts in mind, the clamour for post-Westphalian global democracy appears more like an evasion rather than a confrontation of this reality (Chandler 2010). This conclusion becomes even more apparent when one considers the reactions of advocates of post-Westphalian global democracy to the failure to secure adequate forms of global democracy. For example, Hale et al. (2013) see greater global democracy facing 'gridlock' in the aftermath of the 2008 financial crisis and in response to global problems such as climate change. This is to be explained as the result of growing multipolarity and politicians privileging national over global interests. Habermas (2012) and Beck

(2013) find the Eurozone crisis to be a political rather than economic problem, which stems from national and European elites perpetuating forms of 'post-democratic bureaucratic rule' and the lack of a European identity and public sphere amongst the citizens of European nation states. Bottom-up advocates such as Dryzek (2012) point to the inability of global civil society to achieve significant change at the international level and argue that this reveals the different nature of democracy at the global level in contrast to democracy at the national level.

In seeming to ignore the realm of national democracy in order to argue for global forms of democracy that transcend the state, these authors fail to register how the crisis of democracy at home influences the crisis of democracy abroad. For example, the gridlock facing global multilateralism is not simply a case of growing multipolarity or nationalism amongst politicians but also the hegemony of neoliberalism amongst political elites, anti-cosmopolitanism at home and the fact that countries in the global North are unwilling to cede power within international institutions. The same could be said for the neoliberal settlement that is currently being sought within the Eurozone, where national politicians from northern European countries and elites within institutions, such as the European Central Bank and the IMF, appear to be defending the interests of European finance capital by enforcing austerity on southern European countries (Blyth 2013). This state of affairs remains unchallenged because, as Dryzek (2012) himself laments, the political power associated with global democracy from below is incapable of holding governments to account on such issues.

National democracy and its vitality, as Dewey suggests, is one of the keys to global democracy. Why, for example, are citizens not currently forcing their national representatives to pursue greater multilateralism and cede power at the international level? Why are citizens in northern European states not forcing their governments to back the interests of Europe's citizens rather than its finance capital? Why are global issues such as climate change not key issues for national publics? It is beyond the focus of this present study to offer a full-blown empirical examination of these events but it is safe to say that the answers or at least a large part of the answers to such questions would seemingly revolve around the hegemony of bourgeois democracy and the eclipse of national publics, who are unable to force their political representatives to pursue the democratic way of life both at home and abroad. Moreover, Dewey's work reflects the work of modern writers such as Bandy and Smith (2005: 293, cf. Smith 2008), who upon surveying transnational politics have concluded that the success of global democracy must ' ... rely on well-established national or local movements'. Yet, this perspective is lost in translation when post-Westphalian positions underplay the role of the state and national democracy in the formation of global democracy as a result of the obvious failures of statist positions.

From a Deweyan perspective, the challenge for conceptualizations of global democracy must be to overcome the failings of post-Westphalian ideas of global democracy without having recourse to statist solutions. Rather than abandoning the realm of national democracy and the nation state as defunct political spaces, we must examine the interplay between the present regime of bourgeois democracy at home and the hopes and practice of democracy beyond the nation state. This opens up questions such as: How are our educational and wider cultural practices facilitating global democracy through creating a rooted cosmopolitanism? How are xenophobia and anti-cosmopolitan attitudes linked to income inequality and democratic disillusionment at home? What are the politics and policies through which we can help rediscover the radical faith in democracy and bring forth publics which can exorcise bourgeois democracy at home and abroad? And how is this process helped or hindered by the machinations of globalization and forces outside the state?

These are questions that go beyond mere academic reflection and conjoin with the need for democratic renewal through political activism at the local and national level. As Dewey and his own activism of the 1930s remind us, we must fight for democratic renewal at home to help facilitate democratic renewal abroad. However, what is clear is that the nature, political efficacy or viability, of any conception of 'global democracy' in the twenty-first century can only be adequately conceptualized by revisiting and confronting Deweyan concerns about the political efficacy or viability of publics and their relation to democratic praxis within the nation state. Contrary to post-Westphalian positions on global democracy, the problems of democracy within the nation state cannot be avoided or transcended simply by taking democracy to transnational or global dimensions. Indeed, to phrase the problem in this manner is to miss Dewey's point altogether that without democracy at home there is very little chance of democracy abroad.

Conclusion: Inheriting the Task of Creative Democracy

> *At all events this is what I mean when I say that we now have to re-create by deliberate and determined endeavour the kind of democracy which in its origin one hundred and fifty years ago was largely the product of a fortunate combination of men and circumstances. We have lived for a long time upon that heritage that came to us from the happy conjunction of men and events in an earlier day. The present state of the world is more than a reminder that we have now to put forth every energy of our own to prove worthy of our heritage. It is a challenge to do for the critical and complex conditions of today what the men of an earlier day did for simpler conditions.* (LW14: 225)

The use of historical analogy is always a curious endeavour, as no matter how similar such history is to the present day, the reality is that history, by its very definition, can never be a true reflection of the present. However, maybe the focus on reflection and symmetry is itself a false endeavour and the use of history is best seen as providing extra colour to the spectrum through which we view the present. Just like the death of a dying star light-years away, then, the actual unfolding of events and the lessons to be learnt from the past can only be truly seen long after those events have actually taken place. The life and work of John Dewey would seem to fit this characterization of history. From within our present, Dewey's work, which at its latest point is still over sixty years old, seems to now offer fresh ways of seeing and approaching our contemporary conundrum of managing globalization along democratic lines.

The overriding point of Dewey's work on democracy was that democracy as a way of life, just as other forms of life, was not something that could stand still. The democratic way of life must always move towards meeting those challenges that are present and those that will undoubtedly arise as the conditions of life change (LW13: 299). The democratic ideal therefore always needs updating and unpacking. If democracy were to stand still, it would surrender to circumstance and start on the 'backward road that leads to extinction' (LW11: 182). It was this viewpoint that led Dewey towards becoming a 'global' philosopher and global democrat. This was because Dewey understood that the Great Society and the globalization and scientific revolutions that underpinned it both demanded and offered potential avenues to renew and refresh democracy as a way of life across and between nation states. This held the potential of helping humanity not only move forwards and away from extinction but also move towards a more enhanced and enriched shared existence. This was the dual promise Dewey saw in creative democracy and social intelligence within a global Great Community.

In many ways, this narration of Dewey as a global democrat replicates the contemporary call for the innovation of democracy beyond the state. However, Dewey's work also illuminates the blind spot of our contemporary problematizations of globalization and democracy. This centres on Dewey's idea that democracy is not only simply about governments, states and institutions but a form of life for all of us. It is the spread of democratic habits and dispositions across and between communities that offers us the best chance of renewing and refreshing the democratic ideal in the midst of changing conditions:

> … democracy is a *personal* way of individual life; that it signifies the possession and continual use of certain attitudes, forming personal character and determining desire and purpose in all the relations of life. Instead of thinking of our own disposition and habits as accommodated to certain institutions we have to learn to think of the latter as expressions, projections and extensions of habitually dominant personal attitudes. Democracy as a personal, an individual, way of life involves nothing fundamentally new. But when applied it puts a new practical meaning in old ideas. (LW14: 226)

These words taken from his eightieth birthday address mark out both Dewey's great contribution and challenge as a global philosopher. As this book has tried to show, Dewey's contribution as a global philosopher centres on the theorization of the link between democracy at home and democracy abroad. The formation of the democratic community at the international level is inherently dependant upon the vitality of the community and the diffusion of democratic habits at the national and local level. The possibility of democratic community at the international level is therefore inherently dependant upon the health and status of the democratic community at home. This in turn always takes us back to Dewey's identification of the problem of bourgeois democracy both at home and abroad as the biggest obstacle towards the emergence of creative democracy at home and abroad – a situation that seemingly speaks directly to the social, economic and political contours of our neo-liberal present.

Yet, if Dewey's work brings into analytical focus how the problem of democracy abroad is linked to the problem of bourgeois democracy at home, then his work also challenges us to renew and refresh democracy as a way of life in such circumstances. This is the idea that our democratic inheritance is not static but that:

> ... every generation has to accomplish democracy over again for itself; that its very nature, its essence, is something that cannot be handed on from one person or one generation to another, but has to be worked in terms of needs, problems and conditions of the social life of which, as years go by, we are a part, a social life that is changing with extreme rapidity from year to year. (LW13: 299)

The creative task facing us today very much resembles Dewey's time, in that we need to reformulate democracy in order to cope with the contours of a globalized world. Yes, some of the details may be different. However, when turning to modern issues that demand global democracy, such as climate change and global inequality, it becomes clear that the creative task facing us today is very much the same task that faced Dewey: the eradication of capital's hegemonic control over democratic government and dispelling the political apathy such a state of affairs casts over the masses. Our problem, just like Dewey's, is how to help reorganize the public towards the democratic way of life and the practice of creative democracy. This requires that we recognize that democracy abroad is only possible with democracy at home and that we re-establish what Dewey called the 'fighting faith' of democratic politics. These challenges mark the continuity between Dewey's Great Society and our own present of neo-liberal globalization and also the continuing relevance of Dewey's warning that the failure to meet such a challenge would place humanity further along the road to extinction. For humanity to survive, we must therefore use our democratic inheritance to help us succeed in what Dewey (LW13: 303) called the 'experiment in which we are all engaged, whether we want to be or not, the greatest experiment of humanity', that of living together in ways in which life is profitable in the deepest sense of the word, not just for some, but for all of humanity and the world we inhabit.

Notes

Introduction

1   Citations of John Dewey's works are to *The Collected Works of John Dewey*, edited by Jo Ann Boydston and published by Southern Illinois University Press, 1967–90, and are indicated by EW (*Early Works of John Dewey*), MW (*Middle Works of John Dewey*) or LW (*Later Works of John Dewey*) followed by the respective volume and page numbers.
2   Globalization as a historical process is a much-contested field with estimates of the rise of modern globalization ranging from the eleventh century right up to the nineteenth century. I shall return to the history of globalization and its relationship to Dewey's work in Chapter 2.
3   The main policy recommendations of neo-liberal globalization basically update eighteenth-century economic liberalism with modern-day notions of political democracy and monopoly, for example, patent law. However, neo-liberal globalization is still fundamentally founded on the old liberal's twin belief in the 'efficient market hypothesis' and 'comparative advantage theory'. These two theories, when combined, provide the foundation of the argument that the free market offers maximum economic efficiency and growth, whilst government intervention (capital controls, import quotas, welfare schemes) is harmful because it reduces such competition. Such unhindered competition on a global scale allocates national economies to areas of specialization in which their production techniques are as high in value as possible. For more details on the history of the rise of neo-liberal globalization as a hegemonic economic paradigm and its political implementation, see Harvey (2005), Dumenil and Levy (2004), Blyth (2002) and Frieden (2006), and for an insightful account of the rise of neo-liberalism outside the West, see Prashad (2013).
4   Westbrook's words were undoubtedly aimed at Richard Rorty and his use of Dewey's philosophy. It is beyond doubt that Rorty's *Philosophy and the Mirror of Nature* (1979), more or less, single-handedly revived interest in Dewey's philosophy. However, Rorty's interpretation of Dewey is far from

accepted and has been deemed erroneous by more than one Deweyan scholar (see Westbrook 1991: 540–1, 2005: see Chapter 6 for a summary of the differences between Dewey and Rorty's version of Dewey). Rorty's (1989: 38) response to such criticisms was to argue that he was simply making up 'imaginative playmates' for both himself and his readers and that the accuracy of these playmates to their original inspirations was not important.

Chapter 1

1. I say pretence because America in 1927 cannot be deemed a full democracy in the normal liberal sense because most of its African American population did not possess the ability to participate fully in civil or political life. America became a full liberal democracy only in 1965 with the passing of the Voting Rights Act, which built on the Civil Rights Act of 1964, to stop racist-inspired literacy tests and poll taxes preventing African American citizens from taking up their right to vote.
2. This process was largely achieved through direct state intervention and the 'infant industry' protection devised by Alexander Hamilton and the use of high industrial tariffs – a practice that saw America enforce the highest industrial tariffs of any developed nation right up until 1945. See Chang (2003, 2007) and Lind (2012).
3. For example, whereas prior to 1890 manufacturing could be completed in small factories, after 1890 the average plant size in industries such as automobiles increased immensely. The average car plant in 1909 had around 200 workers and produced ten cars per week; by 1929, this figure had turned into 1,000 workers and more than 400 cars per week. This meant that although in 1929 there were fewer car plants than there had been in 1909, car production in 1929 (5.4 million) far outstripped the 1909 figure (126,000) and the average American worker now produced ten times as many cars (Frieden 2006: 61–3, 161).
4. For Dewey, democratic realism represented a revival of the Platonic notion of philosopher kings, substituting the expert for the philosopher because 'philosophy has become something of a joke, while the image of the specialist, the expert in operation, is rendered familiar

and congenial by the rise of the physical sciences and the conduct of industry' (LW2: 363).

5 Please note that although I shall primarily focus here on Dewey's *The Public and Its Problems* (LW2), when necessary I shall also utilize work that precedes and succeeds the aforementioned title. The reason for doing this, as noted by others such as Kadlec (2007: 100) and Campbell (1995: 147), revolves around the incremental appreciation of economics and politics that Dewey's social philosophy exhibits from the First World War onwards through the Great Depression in works such as *Individualism Old and New* (LW5), *Liberalism and Social Action* (LW11) and the onset of the Second World War in works such as *Freedom and Culture* (LW13). Indeed, Axel Honneth (1998) believes that *The Public and Its Problems* marks a wholesale shift, whereby Dewey throws off his previous Hegelian shackles and finds a more coherent argument to justify democracy. Thus, despite his earlier political radicalism, *The Public and Its Problems* marks a focal point in the trajectory of Dewey's social philosophy.

6 Dewey's conception of individuality as not being originally given but constructed under the influences of associated living is evident from his earliest writings (EW1: 48–9), but finds its most sustained expression in *Human Nature and Conduct* (MW14). For Dewey's take on Darwin's influence on his philosophy, see the essays in MW4 and for his thoughts on William James, see the essay 'The Vanishing Subject in the Psychology of James' (LW14: 155–67).

7 It should also be noted that native biological instincts or impulses are not deemed by Dewey to be non-existent but rather dynamically interpreted and structured into ways of behaving with the environment through habits. For instance, the impulse of hunger does not ordinarily, except in situations of starvation, define the means of its pacification. Rather, the pacification of the impulse is determined through the ways (habits) humans have formed or have found access to food in their environment (See MW14: Chapter 12).

8 The conception of cultural matrix being utilized here originates from *Logic: The Theory of Inquiry* (LW12) and not *The Public and Its Problems*, but its assumptions are easily found throughout Dewey's prior work in general.

9   There are many private associations, such as the family, in which as a society we deem it necessary for public bodies to intervene in (e.g. social/child services). Commentators such as Gouinlock (LW2: xxv) therefore argue that Dewey would have been better off speaking of the problem of regulating the adverse consequences of social behaviour per se. However, as outlined earlier, Dewey does this and more by acknowledging that the very definition of public and private is historically relative, open to contestation and ultimately defined by those within a society. In short, Dewey's position leads us to constantly question the presentation of the public and private, especially any presentation of the public and private as historically static and mutually exclusive spheres.

10 Although Dewey uses the terms 'publics', 'state' and 'government', he points out that these terms are not shackled to modern conceptions of the nation state. As Dewey (LW2: 276n7) points out, 'the text is concerned with modern conditions, but the hypothesis propounded is meant to hold good generally'. The terms 'state', 'government' and 'officer' are therefore freely used by Dewey to denote functions rather than elements distinct to the modern state and could be feasibly used in other contexts. As I shall show in Chapter 5, however, this did not mean that Dewey did not see the historical shackles the nation state seemed to place on publics and how they went about reforming government and the state.

11 As we shall see, Dewey believes that the rate of change of the cultural matrix in industrial/capitalist-based societies is far more pronounced than in the agrarian societies that preceded them. However, the important point here is that Dewey highlights how social change is often differentiated, in its form and intensity, across different relations of associative behaviour (family, school, church, science, art and economic and political relations) rather than mono-causally across the whole of society.

12 As Westbrook (1991: 305) notes, Dewey's use of the '... definite and indefinite articles tended to obscure his contention that in any given society *the* Public was, at most, a collective noun designating plural publics that concerned themselves with the indirect consequences of particular forms of associated activity'.

13 It should be noted here that 'new' public in this context does not necessarily mean that the consequences of associated behaviour in

question are newly created by changes in material aspects of a cultural matrix. It is quite possible for a new public to emerge in response to a change in the cultural foundations, which facilitate a new perception of long-established relations of associative behaviour. It is also possible that a new public may newly reflect the interests of previous older publics who were themselves marginalized or whose grievances were deemed unworthy for public control via government.

14 As Westbrook (1991: 303–5) points out, although Dewey seems to follow pluralism in regarding the state as secondary and functional in response to the interests of publics, it should be noted that he did not see the state as simply balancing the interests of publics. Moreover, Dewey backs the role states could take independent of direct public formation but on the basis that the government and their officers could take actions in the wider interest:

> It is quite true that most states, after they have been brought into being, react upon the primary groupings. When a state is a good state, when the officers of the publics genuinely serve the public interests, the reflex effect is of great importance ... A measure of a good state is the degree to which it relieves individuals from the waste and negative struggle and needless conflict and confesses upon him positive assurance and reinforcement in what he undertakes. (LW2: 280)

Moreover, as we shall see below, this form of state activism only becomes problematic for Dewey when it does not facilitate the ability of publics to democratically challenge or remodel the government and state.

15 There is an obvious link between the power of dominant groups and the ability to control the cultural foundations of a material culture. For instance, it would be very helpful to the interests of dominant groups to have cultural foundations that deem the causes of subordinate groups and their publics as irrational or incorrect and hence unsuited for remaking the state. Dewey is, however, very careful not to fall into a Marxist-style conspiracy narrative that simply equates knowledge as ideology and thus a simple expression of power. Nevertheless, as we shall see, although Dewey never uses the terms 'hegemony' or 'ideological control', he was quite aware of how the interests of dominant groups within society were ultimately refracted through ideas and conceptions of common sense within material culture (LW7: 326).

16 There are some who argue that violence is a legitimate form of politics and in fact is the only way to bring about change within society where there are strongly resistant organized publics. Dewey's reaction to such claims would be to agree with the first statement under certain conditions but to totally dismiss the second statement. Dewey's take on revolutionary violence is driven by a reaction to the argument for violence's historical necessity and an historical appreciation of violence's limits. Dewey's aversion to violence was driven by what he saw in theories such as Marxism, which posited the historical inevitability of violence between two polar classes. This for Dewey seemed illogical because such a dogmatic view of history limits the use of non-violent means a priori. Moreover, Dewey saw revolutionary violence as an option that had become historically discredited and limited. On one hand, Dewey saw history as showing that violence between two groups had produced pyrrhic victories where much that was done had to be done over to restore democracy (LW9: 110–11). On the other hand, the advancement of military technologies meant that the civil or international wars that would see the changeover of power would have the potentiality to ruin all parties and indeed civilization itself. This point itself made it doubly important that violence was seen as means that should be employed only as a last resort (LW11: 55–8). Despite this, and the interpretations that paint him as a card-carrying pacifist, Dewey did not rule out the use of violence altogether. In certain circumstances, and having come via the use of collective and collaborative intelligence rather than sheer dogmatism, Dewey believed that the positive use of force could be pursued (LW14: 75–6).

17 The most sustained narration of Dewey's democracy as a form of 'conflict resolution' is to be found in William R. Caspary's *Dewey on Democracy* (2000). However, Caspary's account, although very good on highlighting Dewey's similarities to contemporary positions of conflict resolution, fails to really get to grips with both the evolutionary nature of Dewey's conception of democracy in response to changes in the global economy and the lessons such work hold in the midst of contemporary economic globalization.

18 Confusingly, across different texts and sometimes within the same text interchangeably, Dewey also uses the terms 'democracy as a social idea', 'method of social intelligence', 'intelligence', 'experimentalist

method', 'collective intelligence', 'co-operative intelligence', 'liberalism' and 'democracy as a way of life' to describe his take on democracy as the best method for dealing with social change. This is because Dewey is describing both an ethical ideal (democracy as a way of life) and a method of value formation (social intelligence) that make up his conception of creative democracy. In Chapter 4, I expand on this method of value formation Dewey called 'social intelligence'. For conceptual clarity, I will henceforth use democracy as a way of life to sum up the ethical commitment Dewey attaches to his idea of creative democracy.

19 The ethical commitment of democracy as a way of life should not be seen as Dewey advocating a formal equality between all opinions. Dewey did, after all, believe in political democracy acting as an intermediary between the democratic ideal and also favoured expert opinion on matters. However, democracy as a way of life looks to ensure the opportunity of all to express their opinion about social institutions so as not repeat the key failure of elitism, whether based on expertise or naked power, which creates a class that is cut off from the concerns of common affairs.

20 As this and the earlier narration of Dewey's conception of the state and publics should make clear, contra James Livingston's (2001: 51–6) otherwise excellent reading of *The Public and Its Problems* as the valorization of cultural politics via an active civil society, Dewey's concept of creative democracy makes distinct claims about the ability of publics to gain access to and modify the state and the political representations of government (LW2: 245–54, 327). The existence of an active civil society of publics is therefore not taken by Dewey to be the ultimate guarantee of having a successful democracy.

21 I use the term 'creative democracy' not only because it best sums up the evolutionary nature of Dewey's idea of democracy but because Dewey himself uses the term to sum up his position in an address given on his eightieth birthday: 'Creative Democracy – The Task Before Us' (LW14: 224–30).

Chapter 2

1 Major studies of Dewey such as Caspary (2000), Hickman (2007), Kadlec (2007) and Westbrook (1991) rarely deal with the global nature

of Dewey's political writings or his political philosophy. For instance, Kadlec (2007) has no real take on Dewey and global democracy. Hickman (2007: 32) acknowledges that Dewey put forward an idea of global citizenship but simply locates this as an earlier account of global civil society. As I show in Chapter 5, this is not entirely what Dewey had in mind. Caspary's study of Deweyan democracy (2000: 3) acknowledges that Dewey wrote about issues of globalization and democracy but then states it will not talk about such issues because they can be detached from an assessment of Dewey's take on democracy. My argument in this chapter, however, is that Deweyan democracy in relation to the Great Society cannot be understood properly without considering issues of globalization and democracy on a global scale. Westbrook (1991) expounds upon Dewey's international writings but he fails to see how globalization and its interplay with national democracy are key to Dewey's ideas of the Great Society and the Great Community.

2 I follow Dani Rodrik (2011) in calling this the First Great Globalization but it should be pointed out that the actual dating of globalization is contested. Janet Abu-Lughod (1989), for instance, traces networks of global connections back to before the 1500s and writers such as Findlay and O'Rourke (2007) and Hopkins (2002) acknowledge earlier forms of globalization. However, as my use of the term 'First Great Globalization' suggests, the form of globalization initiated by the industrial revolution and its technologies is distinct in the way it connected various parts of the world vis-à-vis earlier forms of globalization.

3 Findlay and O'Rourke (2007), for example, call their chapter on the global economy between 1918 and 1939 'De-globalisation'.

4 This folly was at the heart of works, such as *A Tract of Monetary Reform* (1923) and *A Treatise on Money* (1930), where Keynes attempted to point out to policymakers that the gold standard and the policies linked to its maintenance were unsuited to post-war conditions. This was because early twentieth-century capitalism's new structure of corporations, more organized labour markets and the advent of trade unions vis-à-vis independent farmers, small businesses and individual workers meant that the subordination of national economies to the priority of world conditions was now both economic and political dynamite. The details of this great political and economic folly during

the interwar period are covered remarkably well in Ahamed's *Lords of Finance* (2009).

5   There have been some writers such as Cochran (2002, 2010) and Bray (2009, 2011) who have attempted to deal with international ramifications of Dewey's thought. Molly Cochran's work is probably at the foremost of this endeavour and her work has made a valuable contribution through highlighting that Dewey's theory of democracy provides a better approach to democracy at a global level than those mapped out by writers such as Habermas, Dryzek and Held. However, her initial approach was let down by the fact that she viewed Dewey's work as indirectly addressing the global and hence failed to the see how Dewey both espouses global democracy but then questions its feasibility and links this back to domestic politics. In her most recent work, she has attempted to update this position by seemingly acknowledging Dewey's direct confrontation of the problem of globalization and global democracy (see Cochran 2010). However, her work traces Dewey's work only up to the end of the First World War and fails to adequately grasp Dewey's developing thought about the role of nation state in the formation of global democracy. Whilst Cochran rightfully sees Dewey as the resolver of the dualisms that plague the debate about global democracy, her approach fails to adequately see how Dewey believed domestic and global forms of democracy were interlinked and interdependent and how bourgeois democracy at home impinges on democracy abroad (for more on this, see Chapter 5).

6   Dewey refined this position further towards the later years of his life. He saw the melting away of the 'old world' as beginning in the fifteenth century with the discovery, exploration and exploitation of new parts of the world and the concomitant revolution of science, commerce and technology. The 'latter part of the nineteenth century and first decades of the twentieth century' were 'but the physical completion of the expansive movement which for four centuries had first encroaching upon and the breaking down the walls that kept peoples of the earth separate and divided' (LW17: 456).

7   For example, see 'International Co-operation or International Chaos' (LW11: 261–5), 'Contribution to Democracy in a World of Tensions' (LW16), 'What Kind of World Are We Fighting For?' (LW17: 131–2)

8 and the unpublished essays 'World Anarchy or World Order?' (LW15: 204–9) and 'Between Two Worlds' (LW17: 451–65). The international dimensions of Dewey's thought can also be found in major works of this period such as *Freedom and Culture* (LW13).

8 The Mr. Willkie in question here is Wendall Willkie, the Republican nominee for the 1940 general election. Willkie was ultimately defeated by Roosevelt, but he was the author of the 1943 bestseller *One World*, which is part travel monologue detailing his various meetings with global leaders and part political treatise on the need for world government.

9 In this essay, Dewey seems to confuse matters by using the term 'world society' to stand in for Great Community, but his conception of world society is inherently another term for Great Community and should not be seen as breaking the society/community distinction laid out in the previous chapter.

10 Dewey would, for example, lose faith in League of Nations as a vehicle of global democracy as it itself was colonized by the re-emergence of an ever more muscular nationalism and continued Western imperialism. This led to a situation where the League no longer offered the hopes of global democracy but had become a league of governments 'whose policies played a part in bringing on the war and that have no wish to change their policies' (MW15: 378; Westbrook 1991: 262–3). For some this was just the logical conclusion to Dewey's naive backing of American participation in the First World War as part of a wider project of reform both at home and abroad. Moreover, as Cochran (2010: 310) highlights, Dewey's apparent folly and separation of theory and practice has received much scholarly attention. I do not wish to tread over old ground but what is apparent is that Dewey's disillusionment with the post-war settlement should be seen as sign of the old professor learning from his mistakes (see Westbrook 1991: 195–230).

Chapter 3

1 As Leuchtenburg (1993: 200–2) highlights, the prosperity of the 1920s made it seem to some that the United States was achieving the goals of socialism without socialism's means. The Great Society did have some

significant good effects on the lives of ordinary American citizens. The United States in 1928 spent as much on education as the rest of the world; radically improved school and college attendance; cut infant mortality rates by two-thirds; and increased life expectancy for Americans from forty-nine to fifty-nine years. However, as Leuchtenburg goes on to show, these statistics do not touch on the aforementioned racial segregation at the heart of the US life or the fact that material inequality actually increased by the end of 1920s before the onset of the Great Depression. As Livingston (2011: 54) points out, the 1920s saw income shares shift from wages to profits. By 1929, 90 per cent of taxpayers had less disposable income than in 1922, whilst corporate profits rose 63 per cent, dividends doubled and the top 1 per cent of taxpayers increased their disposable income by 63 per cent. In the same period, there had also been a net loss of 1 million manufacturing jobs due to the increased efficiency of technology, which resulted in around a 20 per cent fall in the share of wages in the expenditure of industrial corporations. These numbers seem to bring home Dewey's point that whilst there had been gains for wider society, these changes had been tempered by even wider gains for certain parts of society at the expense of others.

2   Dewey argued that the notion that laissez-faire capitalism equalled the 'philosophy of liberty' was itself incorrect. Such a philosophy failed to acknowledge how 'liberty' was a historically relative concept based on the social conditions of the cultural matrix at a given moment in time. I return to this theme in more depth in Chapter 4.

3   Dewey's belief that the advent of mass communication technology actually helped to create habits, which contributed to the breakdown of the public sphere, places him as a precursor to later media critics ranging from Adorno and Horkhemier and Habermas to the enfant terrible Jean Baudrillard. Even if he was not totally sold on conspiracy narratives of his successors, Dewey recognized what Tim Wu (2011: 6) has recently highlighted, which is that mass communication technologies of the twentieth and early twenty-first centuries have often been brought within the structures of industrial capitalism and had become a 'highly centralized and integrated new industry' in their own right.

4   On this issue, Dewey sounded a warning to the American nation that the country needed to embrace democracy as a way of life and enact creative democracy domestically to deal with the complexity and stratification

he saw within American corporate capitalism and avoid the embrace of the authoritarian politics he associated with fascism, communism and the expert governance of democratic realism. Examples of this train of thought can be found throughout Dewey's work from the 1920s onwards where he puts forward ideas about a form of democratic socialism. Many of Dewey's reforms came to be enshrined in the post-war settlement and the rise of welfare state capitalism in the mid-twentieth century (see Ruggie 1982; Blyth 2002; Harvey 2005). However, it should be pointed out that many of Dewey's reforms were not implemented. Contemporary issues such as the balance between work and leisure, industrial democracy, education provision and the socialization of the economy would benefit from a return to some of the old professor's ideas. I return to this argument in Chapter 4 when I argue that Dewey's idea of creative democracy via social intelligence depends on a radical idea of equality of opportunity and economic outcome.

5   Dewey opposed fascism and communism because they essentially did what corporate America did through substituting a bureaucratic state for big business. As Westbrook (1991: 452) outlines, Dewey thought communism and fascism used violent state power to enforce a form of autocratic corporatism that stifled democracy.

Chapter 4

1   Pappas (2008: 271–2) points out that critics such as Westbrook and Eldridge are fundamentally asking the wrong questions when they seek democratic blueprints from Dewey. This is because Dewey does not want to tell us what to think about democracy but rather how to think democratically. The true lesson of Dewey's work is therefore to be as contextualist as Dewey and examine our own present. I find much to agree with in Pappas, and I would echo his sentiments that critics often ask questions of Dewey that he would have thought rather odd. However, the value of Dewey's work is not simply in teaching us how to think about issues such as global democracy but also centres on important lessons we have seemingly forgotten. As I outline below, Dewey did provide concrete ideas on the future of democracy, which centred on a

critique of capitalism and liberalism's conception of liberty. These ideas were not blueprints but always provisional and subject to their own revision through the process he called social intelligence. However, in the midst of neo-liberal globalization, Dewey's ideas about securing the grounds for the habits of creative democracy and the use of social intelligence may be as pertinent as ever.

2   As Jay Martin (2002: 384) highlights, there are an 'astonishing number of political proposals' that Dewey made during the Depression through his work with the People's Lobby (PL) and the League for Independent Political Action (LIPA) that centred on the economy and politics. This is to say nothing of his earlier co-founding of groups such as the National Association for the Advancement of Colored People (NAACP).

3   Dewey's work has recently been seen as precursor to modern ideas of deliberative democracy (see Putnam 1991, 1994; Westbrook 2005; Kadlec 2007). This idea would have some purchase given Dewey's commitment to communication between publics. However, the key difference centres on Dewey's faith in habits and virtues of social intelligence in comparison to deliberative democratic rules of discourse. For more on the difference between the two approaches, see Pappas (2008: 251–5); and on the differences between Dewey and deliberative democracy's key thinker Jürgen Habermas, see Honneth (1998); Kadlec (2007); Bernstein (2010).

4   As Gouinlock (1972: 345n119) argues, this dependence of the experimental method on evidence does highlight a key role for experts. However, as we encountered in Chapter 1, Dewey argued that a dependence on the evidence of experts was disabling for democracy. The evidence that would be up for debate here would not just be based on the testimony of experts. Gouinlock (1986 cf. Pappas 1998: 252) goes on to highlight that social intelligence would not be solely based on empirical 'facts' but would also incorporate emotions and non-cognitive and non-discursive expressions into the process of co-operative problem solving.

5   This is one of those moments where the ventriloquist must admit to writing his subject's speech for them. Dewey never outlines social intelligence in the systematic way I have done so and my own narration of it owes much to Gouinlock (1972, 1986). The nature of social intelligence is itself an issue of debate. Some Deweyan scholars argue that

Dewey's idea of social intelligence provides an epistemic justification for democracy, predominantly deliberative democracy, over other political regimes (Putnam 1991, 1994; Westbrook 2005: 175–200). In this sense, democracy is justified and most suited to the conditions of the Great Society because it provides the conditions for 'increasing the rationality of solutions to social problems' (Honneth 1998: 773). Others, such as Pappas (2008: see also Gouinlock 1972, 1986; McDermott 2007), have argued that Dewey's work does not pivot on such an epistemic justification of democracy and that Dewey's idea of democracy was more an approach to experience than epistemology.

6   Colin Koopman (2009a), drawing on the work of Livingston (1994, 2001), has written an excellent piece that highlights that this debate about Dewey's political economy seemingly replicates a dualism Dewey would have sought to dismantle. Indeed, Koopman even draws parallels Dewey was unable to see, highlighting the similarities between Hayek and Dewey's thought. Dewey himself might have recoiled at such a contention given his distaste for *The Road to Serfdom* (see Westbrook 1991: 460–1). For Koopman, Dewey's work would undoubtedly lead to the use of both governments and markets to secure democratic aspirations. I think Koopman is generally on the right track here in shifting the debate about Dewey's political economy towards democratic ends. However, I would offer a note of caution about this approach. As I highlight below, Dewey's work reveals significant claims about the role of economic inequality in the perpetuation of bourgeois democracy at home and asymmetric relations between nations. Dewey's work therefore calls for equality of economic outcome to be part of a democratic settlement of the economy. This is based on Dewey's own inquiry into the effect economic inequality has on the democratic way of life. In some ways, the statement that Dewey would utilize both market-based and government means to achieve democratic ends, without really spelling out what those democratic ends entail, doesn't actually get us beyond the dualisms Koopman wishes to negate.

7   At different times, Dewey seems to suggest that laissez-faire liberalism was once a harbinger of liberty and then fell a foul of being ahistorical. This would resemble Dewey's ideas of cultural and institutional 'lag'. However, here and at other times, Dewey suggests that laissez-faire liberalism might have always been unfit for democratic purposes in

the first place. What once may have promised liberty of all through providing an equality of opportunity, unhampered by differences in 'status, birth and family antecedents, and finally, in name at least, of race and sex', during the economic and social conditions of the American frontier had also placed an '… inordinate emphasis upon one aspect of opportunity, namely, upon the narrow phase of economic opportunity which is material and pecuniary'. Dewey argues that the result, which no intelligent observer could deny, was that the eclipse of democratic institutions through inequality was actually the product of the liberty '… which has been striven for and upheld in the name of the maxim of *economic* liberty of the individual' (LW11: 249–50). The chief point here is that Dewey seems to suggest the undemocratic results of laissez-faire liberalism were always going to transpire because the ahistorical ideas of individualism, liberty and democracy that underpin laissez-faire liberalism were always destined to create vast material and cultural conditions of inequality.

8   Dewey never fully explicates how the standard of this equality should be set. His own prescription of reforms to help dismantle the structural inequality of corporate America ranged from the minimum wage, social insurance, higher income tax on high earners and higher corporation tax to all-out federal control and socialization of the economy. However, from his words about the need to at times create 'equalization', Dewey would seemingly leave such a process to the experimental method based on the evidence that significant inequality between individuals and nation states was detrimental to the democratic way of life and should be alleviated. The standards of such equality would have been therefore left up to the practice of social intelligence to formulate. What is important to point out here is that Dewey was not widely legislating or laying down the blueprints for the Great Community but rather conducting his own form of inquiry based on the evidence accrued by himself and others about the nature of liberal capitalism and its ideas of liberty, individualism and equality. These findings could be proven incorrect through further inquiry but appeared provisionally valid, based on evidence to suggest that liberal capitalism and the inequalities it generated were incapable of securing the conditions for creative democracy through the auspices of social intelligence. This view also departs somewhat from Honneth (1998), who seems to argue

that Dewey's sense of economic equality comes from a valorization of an earlier and more just agrarian-based division of labour. This holds some merit but neglects what Livingston (1994) notes is Dewey's understanding of the strengths of the corporate structure and seemingly deposits a primordial conception of economic equality Dewey would have been uncomfortable endorsing. Dewey argued that conditions of modern capitalism demanded a form of economic equality to provide the ethical commitment of democracy as a way of life and for the diffusion of habits of social intelligence. This was not a valorization of the past but more so a reflection upon the needs of the present.

9   The rest of Deen's paper centres on trying to deal with the minimalist arguments about global justice, such as the one advocated by Thomas Nagel (2005). These minimalist conceptions of global justice follow the lead of Rawls (1999) in arguing that the principles of distributive justice only apply to citizens within the same nation state. In Nagel's case, the argument is that justice only exists in the midst of jointly authored coercive institutions that create thick political commitments between citizens. As the global realm does not have these institutions, such as a global state or global citizenship, global justice does not exist and we are therefore confined to a minimal humanitarianism to alleviate absolute poverty. Deen goes through a convoluted process of trying to highlight how a global form of social intelligence would create the very thick political commitments Nagel demands. This inherently gives Nagel too much credit and devalues Dewey's own contribution to this debate. Dewey would have certainly disagreed that the lack of institutions at the global level means that global justice is not possible. Moreover, Dewey took the non-existence of such institutions in the midst of the Great Society to contradict the democratic way of life. This, in turn, called for the creation of such institutions and community rather than providing grounds for the status quo or minimal humanitarianism. In fact, as I show below, Dewey took the context of the Great Society to demand not only such institutions but also a form of economic equality to safeguard the democratic way of life and help facilitate social intelligence across the Great Community.

10 It should be noted that Dewey's work on global democracy following the First World War can be said to harbour Eurocentric ideas, which are rooted in American exceptionalism. However, Dewey's work throughout

the 1920s and 1930s demonstrates a gradual displacing of this idea. Although Dewey places the emphasis here on rich and powerful countries ceding power, he was more than aware that countries which were undergoing imperialism were beginning to exercise their own power and would eventually become key components of the move to force rich and powerful Western nation states to cede power in the global economy (see LW3: 158–62; LW15: 204–9).

11 As I highlight in the next chapter, one of the ways Dewey believed America could help facilitate this process was also by being an example of a successful democracy along the lines of creative democracy and the use of social intelligence. The irony is that throughout the latter half of the twentieth century America has portrayed itself as a successful democracy along lines (liberal capitalist) that Dewey found abhorrent and antithetical to the democratic way of life. Moreover, its use of military force to display its power has been both awe-inspiring and largely self-defeating. Somewhat ironically, Dewey argued against the ability of global hegemon to secure world government through force having seen the rise of Third World nationalism in regions such as Asia (LW15: 204–9).

12 This may give the impression that Dewey saw the natural world as being efficiently utilized. However, it should be noted that Dewey not only saw the incompatibility between bourgeois democracy and democracy as a way of life as centring around the negative effects it had on human lives but also saw the negative effects it had upon the natural world and the environment in which humans lived. Liberal capitalism had seen vast portions of the environment and its natural resources reduced to a 'desert' for future generations, who would have to pay for 'past indulgence in an orgy of so-called economic-liberty' (LW11: 251). Although this book has cast the democratic way of life as concerning the equality of human beings, it has been suggested that Dewey's idea of the democratic way of life seems to posit equality between all existences in nature (Gouinlock 1986; Pappas 2008). This would seemingly remove the hierarchy created between the dualism of man and nature, and lead to an idea that 'every existence deserving the name of existence has something unique and irreplaceable about it' (MW 11:51). As Pappas (2008: 226) notes, this leads to Dewey's position advocating a form of ecological and environmental democracy. It is beyond the scope of this study to flesh

out the contours of Dewey's ecological and environmental democracy beyond saying that ecological concerns would be paramount to how Deweyan democracy would reorient the political economy of liberal capitalism (for more on this strand of Dewey's thought, see Light and Katz 1996; Ralston 2013).

13 There is, of course, a question to be answered here about pluralism and its relationship to Dewey's idea of the Great Community and global democracy. Dewey was convinced of and committed to the idea that the democratic way of life and social intelligence offered America and the world the chance to not only avoid conflict but obtain a more productive form of life. Contemporary pragmatist writers such as Robert Talisse (2007a, 2007b) have argued that this approach makes Dewey's work undemocratic due to an inability to deal with the problem of pluralism. Talisse (2007b: 20–2) begins his argument with the problem John Rawls (1996) called 'reasonable pluralism', that is, 'the view according to which there are several substantive moral visions of the human good that are consistent both with liberal-democratic politics and with the best employment of moral reasoning, but are nonetheless inconsistent with each other'. If we accept this argument, within the democratic order with other fellow citizens who hold moral visions incommensurable with our own, we cannot expect to justify that order and its practices by reference to any common substantive moral vision. Deweyan democracy is therefore both undemocratic and oppressive because it attempts to enlist the coercive power of the state in the task of realizing a set of moral values, democracy as a way of life and social intelligence, which reasonable citizens could reject. Talisse goes on to argue that a combination of a Rawlsian commitment to put substantive moral visions (religious, philosophical) to one side in democratic deliberation and Charles Sanders Pierce's version of pragmatism and its epistemic requirement that all belief aims at truth-apt statements, rather than oppressive Deweyan ideas about democracy as a way of life, provides a conception of pragmatic democracy that can actually deal with the problem of pluralism.

The stakes of such debates have obvious implications for Dewey's ideas about global democracy, whose faith in transnational publics and global institutions is bound to face and elicit competing ideas of the good. However, as Koopman (2009b) argues, the problem of reasonable pluralism is only one way to deal with the problem of pluralism. Dewey's work and his idea of social intelligence takes the problem of pluralism not to mean that we shun our substantive ideas of the good for a thin epistemic proceduralism but that we take the problem of pluralism to orient our substantive normative commitments in the first place. As Koopman (2009b: 62) states, this is:

> ... because conflict over substantive commitments is entirely consistent with Deweyan pluralism in a way that Rawlsian pluralism fails to affirm. The Rawlsian response to pluralism is to rule out a commitment to contentious comprehensive conceptions, which generate conflict. The Deweyan response is to regard pluralism as a condition of politics, which orients or inflects each and every contentious conception that gets put forth, including the contentious conceptions put forth by Deweyans themselves. Whereas Rawls demands that we rule out certain kinds of political commitments, Dewey accepts all comers demanding only that every commitment orient itself as one amidst a plurality of other such commitments. The view motivating the Deweyan approach is that the intractable conflicts generated by pluralism are something we should work with rather than around.

Quite simply, the ethical commitment of democracy as a way of life and the practice of social intelligence would always seek conditions that would allow pluralism to flourish and allow for different viewpoints to put forward their conception of moral value. This would include positions that challenge the ideas of what we take to be the democratic way of life and social intelligence. Indeed, Dewey's arguments about the need for economic equality are based on the need to secure such conditions in order for such a situation to emerge. Dewey did not see the democratic way of life and the use of social intelligence as a coercive and oppressive silencing of pluralism but rather as the most reflexive method to deal with the problem of pluralism and provide a way for different competing ideas of the good to interact, engage and form ways of living together that would be prosperous for all involved. He was quite aware, for example, of the differences between the respective cultural matrices of places such as China, India, Japan, France, Germany, the United Kingdom and the United States without homogenizing these into antagonistic blocs (LW17: 35–6). Thus, one may question if this is actually possible in current circumstances, where the habits of social intelligence are not common and publics appear ever committed to dogmatic forms of moral value. But it seems rather perverse to argue that Deweyan democracy is somehow an oppressive force.

Chapter 5

1. This reflection on the nature of the industrial and complex habits of the Great Society also brings home the fact that just because citizens are conducting complex tasks and have interdependent relations with one another, it does not follow that such habits will produce an understanding of community. Moreover, Dewey's reflections on the division between society and community prefigure Kymlicka's point that a community is not defined by 'the forces people are subject to, but rather how they respond to such forces …' (1999: 437). This also outlines a response to contemporary neo-Marxist critics such as Hardt and Negri (2004), who argue that Dewey's ideas are now outdated and inconsequential because of the rise of information-based and network-based industries. In such a narrative, 'immaterial labour' is said to cultivate co-operative relationships and holds the potential to see the rise of the 'multitude' across the globe. Dewey would have been sceptical of such a rewriting of the Marxist narrative, however, because of the fact that the industrial and technological revolutions of his age also created large swathes of co-operative relationships. There is a distinct difference, something Hardt and Negri fail to realize, between what Dewey saw as physical interdependence and moral co-operation.
2. The spread of such nationalism outside of the West and into regions such as Asia also brought home for Dewey that the age of European imperialism was now over and that the idea of a global military hegemon was also unfeasible. Dewey thus understood in 1946 the ramifications of what was to become known as 'Third World Nationalism' and no doubt would have recoiled in horror had he had lived to see the Vietnam War and other countless apparent interventions in the Third World by the United States and Western countries throughout the Cold War and beyond (See LW3: 159; LW15: 208).

3   It is also important, however, to note that the above does not commit the reverse sin of reifying the nation state, nationalism and nation state politics at the expense of the global or transnational. The irony of Dewey's position is that it refutes essentialism but deals with the harsh reality of such anti-essentialism. Although embracing anti-essentialist conceptions of the public, state and government, which do not exclusively link those concepts and functions with the nation state, Dewey's view seems to posit that the emergence of the nation state and nationalism places a historically contingent limit on the nature of global democracy. It may very well be that eventually the nation states and nationalism cease to be as important or even disappear. However, in Dewey's eyes, the nation state and nationalism were to be taken very much like solid brick walls: whilst they are undoubtedly constructions, one would be very hard-headed to believe that one could simply walk through them.

4   Dewey's focus on the face-to-face communication and his claim that the Great Community would not have the same intimacy of communication as the local setting has been presented as the ramblings of an old man with a rose-tinted nostalgia for a form of localism lost to the confines of history (see Westbrook 1991; Ryan 1995; Cochran 2002). This in turn has often clouded assessments of Dewey's global thought. However, as my exposition highlights, this is actually far from the truth. The local community was important for Dewey but only as a reconstructed local community within the Great Community at both national and international level. Indeed, such nostalgia for earlier, and so-called 'simpler' times, made Dewey downhearted: 'I find myself resentful and feeling sad when, in relation to present social, economic, and political problems, people point simply backward as if somewhere in the past there were a model for what we should do today' (LW 13: 299).

5   One could argue that Dewey's work prefigures a form of cosmopolitan nationalism as outlined by writers such as Eckerlsey (2007) and Tan (2008). Whilst there are similarities to such approaches, the key difference between Dewey and writers such as Tan is that Dewey does not adhere to two-stage process where democracy within the state must be obtained before democracy beyond the state can even be contemplated. Whereas Dewey saw democracy at home as key to

securing democracy abroad, the fact was that securing the democratic way of life was not simply about choosing respective focal points of political action such as the local, national or global. Rather, the struggle for democracy as a way of life was to be '... maintained on as many fronts as culture has aspects: political, economic, international, educational, scientific and artistic, religious' (LW13: 186).

6 It should be noted that this adage that democracy must begin at home would also stand for countries that are economically weaker and under the coercion of stronger nations or who find themselves under undemocratic conditions in the first instance. Without democracy at home, any movement for freedom would be bound to end in ruins. History would see this unfold after Dewey's death with the rise and fall of the Third World project. Whilst the new postcolonial states of Africa, Asia and Latin America forged some of the most coherent policies for regulating the global economy in democratic terms, two assailants assassinated the movement. The first was the continued informal economic and political imperialism, what we today call neo-imperialism, conducted by Western nations against their former colonies. The second factor was the failure of elites within such new countries to create stable democracies in the midst of such conditions. Whilst these elites can rightfully shift some of the blame to factors outside their borders, it was also the failure of such dominant classes to create a vibrant democracy at home that led to collapse of the rooted cosmopolitanism at the heart of the Third World project and the rise of the destructive and divisive cultural nationalism that followed. For greater details on this, see Prashad (2008, 2013).

7 This point also highlights how Bray's (2009, 2011, 2013) attempt to reorient modern cosmopolitanism to a form of pragmatic cosmopolitanism undersells the power of Dewey's work on global democracy. Bray's argument is that Dewey's work on publics opens up the chance to bypass the ethnocentrism of modern cosmopolitanism. This would see the 'hardwiring' of cosmopolitanism into the attitudes of citizens through practices and institutions such as education. The hope being that such practices could facilitate the emergence of citizens and publics who would implore and force their leaders to create a 'self-sacrificing nation committed to foreign aid and global justice' (Bray 2013:

462–3). Bray does suggest, however, that Dewey is too naive about how such a process could come about in an economically stratified society and unprepared to face up to the real obstacles of asymmetrical power relations facing the pursuit of the democratic way of life both within and beyond the nation state (Bray 2011: 160–2). The main problem is that Bray's portrayal of Dewey as being politically naive on issues of power neglects Dewey's problematic of bourgeois democracy and his appreciation of the stratified nature of the global economy. Indeed, Bray seemingly neglects how Dewey's problematic of bourgeois democracy complicates his own idea of creating cosmopolitan leadership at the national level. In doing this, Bray fails to grasp Dewey's key intervention on global democracy, which located the hopes and aspirations of democracy abroad with the challenge of destroying bourgeois democracy at home.

8 This point marks out a significant moment where Dewey failed to consistently apply his own philosophy to some of his insights. Much like Karl Polanyi, Dewey seems to have become fixated on the British Labour Party as embodying the type of democratic socialism he envisioned. However, whilst being more progressive than Roosevelt and the New Deal, Dewey seems blind to the fact that, based upon his own criteria, Attlee's government did not practise creative democracy at home or abroad. As Dale (2010: 205) outlines, the post-war Labour government did not represent a wholesale rejection of market capitalism but rather a continuation of the liberal-imperialist agenda that came beforehand. This is evidenced by the post-war Labour government's continuance of the British Empire and its secret nuclear weapon programme. In short, the Atlee government may have pursued some elements of democratic socialism at home but it was not an example of the rooted cosmopolitanism and form of democratic socialism Dewey imagined both at home and abroad.

9 Mazower (2012) provides an excellent account of the travails of extending democracy beyond the nation state throughout Dewey's lifetime and beyond. For a view of such events from outside of the Anglo and European world, see Vijay Prashad's wonderful history of the Third World project (2008, 2013).

10 The demise of old economic liberalism and the rise of neo-liberalism sandwich the period now known as 'embedded liberalism'. This saw the post-war international monetary system facilitate the emergence of 'embedded liberal states', or what we commonly see as modern welfare states and perhaps the most productive and fairly distributed form of capitalism ever known (Ruggie 1983; Blyth 2002; Harvey 2005; Frieden 2006; Rodrik 2011). I do not have the space here to expand on this but Dewey would have seen great promise and great flaws in such a regime. The proof of this resides in his critique of the New Deal, which can be seen as a precursor to the modern welfare states of the embedded liberal period. Dewey would have seen the move towards a more regulated form of capitalism as only a half-way house towards securing the equality of opportunity needed to secure the democratic way of life both at home and abroad because of the persistence of large-scale economic inequalities. What is needed is not just a fairer capitalism for a brief period but a fair social economic system that can be productive in terms of both economic output and human development.

11 This analogy becomes even more pertinent when one considers the levels of wealth inequality in neo-liberal hotbeds such as the United States and the United Kingdom. As Wade (2009b: 541) outlines, the Reagan/Thatcher policy changes were phenomenally successful, helping to produce the biggest upwards redistribution in the West in over a century. From 1980, the share of the top 1 per cent in the United States took off like a rocket to regain by 2006 its 1929 peak.

Bibliography

Abu-Lughod, J. (1989), *Before European Hegemony: The World System A.D. 1250–1350*. Oxford: Oxford University Press.
Adorno, T. (1973), *Negative Dialectics*. New York: Continuum Press.
Ahamed, L. (2009), *Lords of Finance*. London: Windmill Books.
Anderson, B. (1991), *Imagined Communities*. London: Verso.
Appiah, K.W. (1996), 'Cosmopolitan Patriots', in J. Cohen (ed.) *For the Love of Country*. Boston, MA: Beacon Press.
Appiah, K.W. (2005), *The Ethics of Identity*. Princeton, NJ: Princeton University Press.
Archibugi, D. (2008), *The Global Commonwealth of Citizens: Toward Cosmopolitan Democracy*. Princeton, NJ: Princeton University Press.
Bandy, J. and Smith, J. (eds.) (2005), *Coalitions Across Borders: Transnational Protest and the Neo-Liberal Order*. Lantham, MD: Rowman and Littlefield.
Beck, U. (2013), *German Europe*. Cambridge: Polity Press.
Bello, W. (2005), *Deglobalization Ideas for a New World Economy*. London: ZED Books.
Bello, W. (2013), *Capitalism's Last Stand: Deglobalization in the Age of Austerity*. London: Zed Books.
Bernstein, R.J. (2010), *The Pragmatic Turn*. Cambridge: Polity Press.
Bhambra, G.K. (2011), 'Cosmopolitanism and the Postcolonial Critique', in M. Nowicka and M. Rovisco (eds.) *The Ashgate Research Companion to Cosmopolitanism*. Aldershot: Ashgate, pp. 313–28.
Billig, M. (1995), *Banal Nationalism*. London: Sage Publications.
Blyth, M. (2002), *Great Transformations: Economic Ideas and Institutional Change in the Twentieth Century*. Cambridge: Cambridge University Press.
Blyth, M. (2013), *Austerity: The History of a Dangerous Idea*. Oxford: Oxford University Press.
Bohman, J. (2007), *Democracy Across Borders: From Demos to Demoi*. Cambridge: MIT Press.
Brassett J. and Smith, W. (2010), 'Deliberation and Global Civil Society: Agency, Arena, Affect', *Review of International Studies*, 36(2): 413–30.
Bray, D. (2009), 'Pragmatic Cosmopolitanism: A Deweyan Approach to Democracy beyond the Nation-State'. *Millennium: Journal of International Studies*, 37(3): 683–719.

Bray, D. (2011), *Pragmatic Cosmopolitanism: Representation and Leadership in Transitional Democracy*. London: Palgrave Macmillan

Bray, D. (2013), 'Pragmatic Ethics and the Will to Believe in Cosmopolitanism', *International Theory*, 5(3): 446–76.

Brown, G.W. and Held, D. (2010), *The Cosmopolitanism Reader*. Cambridge: Polity Press.

Calhoun, C. (2008), *Nations Matter: Culture, History, and the Cosmopolitan Dream*. New York: Routledge.

Calhoun, C. (2010), 'Beck, Asia and Second Modernity', *British Journal of Sociology*, 61(3): 597–617.

Campbell, J. (1995), *Understanding John Dewey*. Chicago: Open Court.

Caspary, W.R. (2000), *Dewey on Democracy*. Ithaca, NY and London: Cornell University Press.

Chandler, D. (2010), *Hollow Hegemony: Rethinking Global Politics, Power and Resistance*. London: Pluto.

Chang, H.J. (2003), *Kicking Away the Ladder: Development Strategies in Historical Perspective*. London: Anthem.

Chang, H.J. (2007), *Bad Samaritans*. London: Random House.

Cochran, M. (2001), 'A Pragmatist Perspective on Ethical Foreign Policy', in K. Smith and M. Light (eds.) *Ethics and Foreign Policy*. Cambridge: Cambridge University Press, pp. 55–72.

Cochran, M. (2002), 'A Democratic Critique of Cosmopolitan Democracy: Pragmatism from the Bottom-Up', *European Journal of International Relations*, 8(4): 517–48.

Cochran, M. (ed.) (2010), *The Cambridge Companion to Dewey*. New York: Cambridge University Press.

Dahl, R. (1999), 'Can International Organizations be Democratic? A Skeptical View', in I. Shapiro and C. Hacker-Cordon (eds.) *Democracy's Edges*. New York: Cambridge University Press.

Dahl, R. (2001), 'Is Post-National Democracy Possible?', in S. Fabbrini (ed.) *Nation, Federalism and Democracy*. Trento: Editrice Compositori.

Dale, G. (2010), *Karl Polanyi: The Limits of the Market*. Cambridge: Polity Press.

Deen, P. (2013), 'Justice and Global Communities of Inquiry', in S.J. Ralston (ed.) *Pragmatism and International Relations: Essays for a New Bold World*. Plymouth: Lexington Books.

Dewey, J. (EW1), 'Early Essays and Leibniz's New Essays', in J. Boydston (ed.) *John Dewey The Early Works 1882–1898, Volume 1: 1882–1888*. Carbondale: Southern Illinois University Press.

Dewey, J. (MW4), 'Journal Articles and Book Reviews in the 1907–1909 Period, and The Pragmatic Movement of Contemporary Thought and Moral Principles in Education', in J. Boydston (eds.) *John Dewey The Middle Works 1899–1924, Volume 4: 1907–1909*. Carbondale: Southern Illinois University Press.

Dewey, J. (MW9), 'Democracy and Education', in J. Boydston (ed.) *John Dewey The Middle Works 1899–1924, Volume 9: 1916*. Carbondale: Southern Illinois University Press.

Dewey, J. (MW10), 'Journal Articles, Essays and Miscellany', in J. Boydston (ed.) *John Dewey The Middle Works 1899–1924, Volume 10: 1916–1917*. Carbondale: Southern Illinois University Press.

Dewey, J. (MW11), 'Journal Articles, Essays and Miscellany', in J. Boydston (ed.) *John Dewey The Middle Works 1899–1924, Volume 11: 1918–1919*. Carbondale: Southern Illinois University Press.

Dewey, J. (MW12), 'Reconstruction in Philosophy', in J. Boydston (ed.) *John Dewey The Middle Works 1899–1924, Volume 12: 1920*. Carbondale: Southern Illinois University Press.

Dewey, J. (MW14), 'Human Nature and Conduct', in J. Boydston (ed.) *John Dewey The Middle Works 1899–1924, Volume 14: 1922*. Carbondale: Southern Illinois University Press.

Dewey, J. (MW15), 'Journal Articles, Essays and Miscellany', in J. Boydston (ed.) *John Dewey The Middle Works 1899–1924, Volume 15: 1923–1924*. Carbondale: Southern Illinois University Press.

Dewey, J. (LW1), 'Experience and Nature', in J. Boydston (ed.) *John Dewey The Later Works 1925–1953, Volume 1: 1925*. Carbondale: Southern Illinois University Press.

Dewey, J. (LW2), 'The Public and Its Problems', in J. Boydston (ed.) *John Dewey The Later Works 1925–1953, Volume 2: 1925–27*. Carbondale: Southern Illinois University Press.

Dewey, J. (LW3), 'Essays, Reviews, and Miscellany and Impressions of Soviet Russia', in J. Boydston (ed.) *John Dewey The Later Works 1925–1953, Volume 2: 1925–27*. Carbondale: Southern Illinois University Press.

Dewey, J. (LW5), 'Individualism Old and New', in J. Boydston (ed.) *John Dewey The Later Works 1925–1953, Volume 5: 1929–30*. Carbondale: Southern Illinois University Press.

Dewey, J. (LW6), 'Essays, Reviews, and Miscellany', in J. Boydston (ed.) *John Dewey The Later Works 1925–1953, Volume 6: 1931–32, 131–32*. Carbondale: Southern Illinois University Press.

Dewey, J. (LW7), 'Ethics', in J. Boydston (ed.) *John Dewey The Later Works 1925–1953, Volume 7: 1932.* Carbondale: Southern Illinois University Press.

Dewey, J. (LW9), 'A Common Faith', in J. Boydston (ed.) *John Dewey The Later Works 1925–1953, Volume 9: 1933–34.* Carbondale: Southern Illinois University Press.

Dewey, J. (LW11), 'Liberalism and Social Action', in J. Boydston (ed.) *John Dewey The Later Works 1925–1953, Volume 11: 1935.* Carbondale: Southern Illinois University Press.

Dewey, J. (LW13), 'Freedom and Culture', in J. Boydston (ed.) *John Dewey The Later Works 1925–1953, Volume 13: 1938–1939.* Carbondale: Southern Illinois University Press.

Dewey, J. (LW14), 'Essays, Reviews, and Miscellany', in J. Boydston (ed.) *John Dewey The Later Works 1925 –1953, Volume 14: 1939–1941.* Carbondale: Southern Illinois University Press.

Dewey, J. (LW15), 'Essays, Reviews, and Miscellany', in J. Boydston (ed.) *John Dewey The Later Works 1925–1953, Volume 15: 1942–1948.* Carbondale: Southern Illinois University Press.

Dewey, J. (LW16), 'Essays, Typescripts, and Knowing and the Known', in J. Boydston (ed.) *John Dewey The Later Works 1925–1953, Volume 16: 1949–1952.* Carbondale: Southern Illinois University Press.

Dewey, J. (LW17), 'Essays, Reviews, and Miscellany', in J. Boydston (ed.) *John Dewey The Later Works 1925–1953, Volume 17: 1885–1953.* Carbondale: Southern Illinois University Press.

Dryzek, J. (2006), *Deliberative Global Politics: Discourse and Democracy in a Divided World.* Cambridge: Polity Press.

Dryzek, J. (2010), *Foundations and Frontiers of Deliberative Governance.* Oxford: Oxford University Press.

Dryzek, J. (2012), 'Global Civil Society: The Progress of Post-Westphalian Politics', *Annual Review of Political Science*, 15: 101–19.

Duménil, G. and Lévy, D. (2004), *Capital Resurgent: Roots of the Neo-Liberal Revolution.* London: Harvard University Press.

Eckerlsey, R. (2007), 'From Cosmopolitan Nationalism to Cosmopolitan Democracy', *Review of International Studies*, 33: 675–92.

Eldridge, M. (1998), *Transforming Experience: John Dewey's Cultural Instrumentalism.* Nashville: Vanderbilt University Press.

Englen, E., Erturk, I., Froud, J., Johal, S., Leaver, A., Moran, M., Nilson, A., and Williams, K. (2011), *After the Great Complacence: Financial Crisis and the Politics of Reform.* Oxford: Oxford University Press.

Findlay, R. and O.Rourke, K.H. (2007), *Power and Plenty: Trade, War, and the World Economy in the Second Millennium*. Princeton, NJ: Princeton University Press.

Fine, R. (2007), *Cosmopolitanism*. Abingdon: Routledge.

Frieden, J.A. (2006), *Global Capitalism: Its Rise and Fall in the Twentieth Century*. New York: Norton.

Gilens, M. (2012), *Affluence and Influence: Economic Inequality and Political Power in America*. Princeton, NJ: Princeton University Press.

Gouinlock, J. (1972), *John Dewey's Philosophy of Value*. New York: Humanities.

Gouinlock, J. (1986), *Excellence in Public Discourse: John Stuart Mill, John Dewey and Social Intelligence*. New York: Teachers College Press.

Gouinlock, J. (1990), 'What Is the Legacy of Instrumentalism? Rorty's Interpretation of Dewey', *Journal of the History of Philosophy*, 28(2): 251–69.

Habermas, J. (2001), *The Post-National Constellation*. Cambridge: Polity Press.

Habermas, J. (2006), *The Divided West*. Cambridge: Polity Press.

Habermas, J. (2012), *The Crisis of the European Union*. Cambridge: Polity Press.

Hale, T., Held, D., and Young, K. (2013), *Gridlock: Why Global Cooperation Is Failing When We Need It Most*. Cambridge: Polity Press.

Hardt, M. and Negri, A. (1999), *Empire*. London: Harvard University Press.

Hardt, M. and Negri, A. (2004), *Multitude: War and Democracy in the Age of Empire*. London: Penguin Books.

Hardt, M. and Negri, A. (2011), 'The Fight for Real Democracy at the Heart of Occupy Wall Street', *Foreign Affairs*, www.foreignaffairs.com/articles/136399/michael-hardt-and-antonio-negri/the-fight-for-real-democracy-at-the-heart-of-occupy-wall-street (accessed 4 April 2014).

Harvey, D. (2005), *A Brief History of Neoliberalism*. Oxford: Oxford University Press.

Hay, C. (2007), *Why We Hate Politics*. Cambridge: Polity Press.

Heidegger, M. (1977), *The Question Concerning Technology and Other Essays*. New York: Harper and Row.

Held, D. (1995), *Democracy and the Global Order*. Cambridge: Polity Press.

Held, D. (2004), *Global Covenant: The Social Democratic Alternative to the Washington Consensus*. Cambridge: Polity Press.

Held, D. (2010), *Cosmopolitanism*. Cambridge: Polity Press.

Held, D. and McGrew, A. (2007), *Globalization/Anti-Globalization*. Cambridge: Polity Press.

Hickman, L. (2007), *Pragmatism as Post-Postmodernism: Lessons from John Dewey*. New York: Fordham University Press.

Hirst, P., Thompson, G., and Bromley, S. (2009), *Globalization in Question: The International Economy and the Possibilities of Governance*. Cambridge: Polity Press.

Hobson, J.M. (2012), *The Eurocentric Conception of World Politics: Western International Theory 1760 –2010*. Cambridge: Cambridge University Press.

Honneth, A. (1998), 'Democracy as Reflexive Cooperation', *Political Theory*, 26(6), 763–83.

Hopkins, A.G. (2002), 'The History of Globalization – and the Globalization of History', in A.G. Hopkins (ed.) *Globalization in World History*. London: Pimlico.

Horkheimer, M. (1972), *Critical Theory*. Trans. Mathew J. O'Connel. New York: Continuum Press.

Kadlec, A. (2007), *Dewey's Critical Pragmatism*. Lanham, MD: Lexington Books.

Kaldor, M. (2003), *Global Civil Society: An Answer to War*. Cambridge: Polity Press.

Keck, M. and Sikkink K. (1998), Activists *Beyond Borders*. Ithaca, NY: Cornell University Press.

Kennedy, P. (1987), *The Rise and Fall of the Great Powers*. New York: Random House.

Keynes, J.M. (1919), *The Economic Consequences of the Peace*. New York: Harcourt Brace.

Keynes, J.M. (1923), *A Tract on Monetary Reform*. London: Mcmillan.

Keynes, J.M. (1930), *A Treatise on Money*. London: Mcmillan.

Kloppenberg, J.T. (1986), *Uncertain Victory: Social Democracy and Progressivism in European and American Thought: 1870–1920*. Oxford: Oxford University Press.

Kloppenburg, J.T. (1994), 'Democracy and Disenchantment: From Weber and Dewey to Habermas and Rorty', in D. Ross (ed.) *Modernist Impulses in the Human Sciences*. Baltimore, MD: Johns Hopkins University Press, pp. 69–90.

Koopman C. (2009a), 'Morals and Markets: Liberal Democracy through Dewey and Hayek', *Journal of Speculative Philosophy*, 23(3): 151–79.

Koopman, C. (2009b), 'Good Questions and Bad Answers in Talisse's A Pragmatist Philosophy of Democracy', *Transactions of the Charles S. Peirce Society: A Quarterly Journal in American Philosophy*, 45(1): 60–4.

Kymlicka, W. (1999), 'Citizenship in an Era of Globalization: Commentary on Held', in I. Shapiro and C. Hacker-Cordon (eds.) *Democracy's Edges*. New York: Cambridge University Press.

Leuchtenburg, W. (1993), *The Perils of Prosperity: 1914–32*. Chicago: Chicago Press.

Lind, M. (2012), *Land of Promise: An Economic History of the American Economy*. New York: HarperCollins.

Light, A. and Katz, E. (eds.) (1996), *Environmental Pragmatism*. New York: Routledge.

Lippmann, W. (1922), *Public Opinion*. New York: Free Press.

Lippmann, W. (1925), *The Phantom Public*. New York: Transaction Publishers.

Livingston, J. (1994), *Pragmatism and the Political Economy of Cultural Revolution, 1850–1940*. Chapel Hill: University of North Carolina.

Livingston, J. (2001), *Pragmatism, Feminism, and Democracy: Rethinking the Politics of American History*. New York: Routledge.

Livingston, J. (2011), *Against Thrift*. New York: Basic Books.

Lukacs, G. (1971), *History and Class Consciousness: Studies in Marxist Dialectics*. Trans. Rodeny Livingston. Cambridge: MIT Press.

Martin, J. (2002), *The Education of John Dewey*. New York: Columbia University.

Mazower, M. (2012), *Governing the World: A History of an Idea*. London: Penguin Books.

McDermott, J. (2007), *The Drama of Possibility: Experience as Philosophy*. New York: Fordham University Press.

Mead, G.H. (1915), 'Natural Rights and the Theory of Political Institution', *The Journal of Philosophy, Psychology and Scientific Methods*, 12(6): 141–55.

Mills, C.W. (1964), *Sociology and Pragmatism: Higher Learning in America*. New York: Paine Whitman Publishers.

Morris, I. (2011), *Why the West Rules for Now: Patterns of History and What It Reveals about the Future*. London: Profile Books.

Mosley, L. (2005), 'Globalization and the State: Still Room to Move?', *New Political Economy*, 10(3): 355–62.

Mumford, L. (1926), *The Golden Day: A Study in American Experience and Culture*. New York: Horace Liveright.

Nagel, T. (2005), 'The Problem of Global Justice', *Philosophy and Public Affairs*, 33(2): 113–47.

Niebuhr, R. (1932), *Moral Man and Immoral Society*. New York: Scribners.

Pappas, G.F. (2008), *John Dewey's Ethics: Democracy as Experience*. Bloomington: Indiana University Press.
Patomäki, H. (2011), 'Towards Global Political Parties', *Ethics and Global Politics*, 4(2): 81–102.
Prashad, V. (2008), *The Darker Nations: A People's History of the Third World*. New York: The New Press.
Prashad, V. (2013), *The Poorer Nations: A Possible History of The Global South*. London: Verso.
Putnam, H. (1991), 'A Reconsideration of Deweyan Democracy', in M. Brint and W. Weavers (eds.) *Pragmatism in Law and Society*. Boulder, CO: Westview Press, pp. 217–42.
Putnam, H. (1994), *Words and Life*. Cambridge: Harvard University Press.
Ralston, S.J. (2013), *Environmental Pragmatism*. Leicester: Troubadour Publishing.
Rao, R. (2010), *Third World Protest: Between Home and the World*. Oxford: Oxford University Press.
Rawls, J. (1996), *Political Liberalism*. New York: Columbia University Press.
Rawls, J. (1999), *The Law of Peoples*. Cambridge: Harvard University Press.
Rodrik, D. (2011), *The Globalisation Paradox: Democracy and the Future of the World Economy*. London: Norton.
Rodrik, D. (2012), 'The Nation State Reborn', *Project Syndicate*, 13 February 2012, www.project-syndicate.org/commentary/the-nation-state-reborn (accessed 4 April 2014).
Rorty, R. (1979), *Philosophy and the Mirror of Nature*. Princeton, NJ: Princeton University Press.
Rorty, R. (1989), 'Philosophy of the Oddball', *New Republic*, 19 June 1989.
Rorty, R. (1998), *Truth and Progress: Philosophical Papers: Volume 3*. Cambridge: Cambridge University Press.
Rorty, R. (1999), *Achieving Our Country: Leftist Thought in the Twentieth Century*. Cambridge: Harvard University Press.
Ruggie, J.G. (1982), 'International Regimes, Transactions and Change: Embedded Liberalism in the Postwar Economic Order', *International Organization*, 36(Spring): 557–83.
Russell, B. (1909), *Philosophical Essays*. New York: Simon and Schuster.
Russell, B. (1922), 'As a Radical European Sees It', *Freeman*, 4: 608–10.
Ryan, A. (1995), *John Dewey and the High Tide of American Liberalism*. New York: W.W. Norton

Scholte, J. (2012), 'Reinventing Global Democracy', *European Journal of International Relations*, first published online 29 May 2012.

Sen, J. and Escobar, A. (eds.) (2007), *World Social Forum*. New Delhi: Viveka Foundation.

Smith, J. (2008), *Social Movements for Global Democracy*. Baltimore, MD: John Hopkins University Press.

Smith, W. and Brassett, J. (2008), 'Deliberation and Global Governance: Liberal, Cosmopolitan and Critical Perspectives', *Ethics and International Affairs*, 22(1): 69–92.

Stiglitz, J.E. (2010), *Freefall: Free Markets and the Sinking of the Global Economy*. London: Penguin Books.

Stiglitz, J.E. (2012), *The Price of Inequality*. London: Alan Lane.

Talisse, R.B. (2007a), *A Pragmatist Philosophy of Democracy*. New York: Routledge

Talisse, R.B. (2007b), 'Two Democratic Hopes', *Contemporary Pragmatism*, 4(2): 19–28.

Tan, K.C. (2008), 'Global Democracy: International, Not Cosmopolitan', in D.K. Chatterjee (ed.) *Democracy in a Global World*. Lanham, MD: Rowman & Littlefield, pp. 161–83.

Tarrow, S. (2005), *The New Transnational Activism*. Cambridge: Cambridge University Press.

Tarrow, S. (2011), *Power in Movement*. Cambridge: Cambridge University Press.

Wade, R. (2009a), 'Is the Globalisation Consensus Dead?', *Antipode*, 41(S1): 142–65.

Wade, R. (2009b), 'From Global Imbalances to Global Reorganizations', *Cambridge Journal of Economics*, 33(4): 539–62.

Wade, R. (2012), 'Why Has Income Inequality Remained on the Sidelines of Public Policy for So Long', *Challenge*, 55(6): 21–50.

Wade, R. (2013), 'The Art of Power Maintenance: How Western States Keep the Lead in Global Organizations', *Challenge*, 56(1): 5–39.

Wallas, G. (1914), *The Great Society*. London: Allen and Unwin.

Weiss, L. (2009), 'The State in the Economy: Neoliberal or Neoactivist?', in J. Campbell et al. (eds.) *Oxford Handbook of Comparative Institutional Analysis*. Oxford: Oxford University Press.

West, C. (1989), *The American Evasion of Philosophy: A Genealogy of Pragmatism*. Madison: University of Wisconsin Press.

Westbrook, R. (1991), *John Dewey and American Democracy*. New York: Cornell University Press.

Westbrook, R. (2005), *Democratic Hope*. Ithaca, NY: Cornell University Press.

Wu, T. (2011), *The Master Switch: The Rise and Fall of Information Empires*. New York: Vintage Books.

Index

Note: locators followed by 'n' indicate notes section

Abu-Lughod, J. 138
Adorno, T. 75, 141 n.3
agrarian-based division of labour 146 n.8
Ahamed, L. 139 n.4
American Civil War 3, 16
American Friends for Spanish Democracy 121
Americanism 2
American pragmatism 2
Anderson, B. 108
animal rights 26
antagonism 71, 98, 107
anti-cosmopolitanism 124
anti-essentialism 107, 151 n.3
anti-globalization movement 7
Appiah, K. W. 121
Archibugi, D. 7
associated human behaviour, observation of the consequences 29
associative behaviour 23–7, 29–30, 34–5, 57
  consequences of 24–6, 48
  incorrect perceptions of 29
  private transactions of 24
atomic age, rise of 50
atomic bomb, global ramifications of 3
autarky 45, 49, 72, 107
Axis Powers 49

Bandy, J. 125
Basel Committee 122
Battle of Fort Sumter 1
Beck, U. 123
Bello, W. 8

Bernstein, R. J. 2, 75, 112, 143 n.3
Bhambra, G. K. 7
Billig, M. 108
Blyth, M. 124, 131 n.3, 142 n.4, 154 n.10
bourgeois democracy 11–12, 59–60, 67–73, 76, 85–9, 100, 115–20, 123, 125
  advent of 90
  artificial intellectual inequality 66
  confines of 61, 68, 97
  control of the Great Society 71
  cultural inequalities 115–16
  cultural reorganization 118
  economic stratification 70
  educative rhythm of creative democracy 69
  failings of 72
  free speech, free press and free assembly 65
  hegemony of 60–1, 71, 73, 117, 125
  inequality 69, 72
  influence on global democracy 115
  intellectual inequality 116
  intellectual stratification 70
  liberal capitalism and 100
  material inequality 115–16
  political economy 86, 118
  political reorganization 118
  problem of 104, 115, 120, 129
  relation with global democracy 116
  sporadic reforms 86
  stratification of 69, 72
  structural inequalities of 116

Brassett J. 7
Bray, D. 139 n.5, 152–3 n.7
Brazil 122
Bretton Woods regime 1
Britain
  as biggest economy in the world 16
  gold standard 42, 44
  political engagement 44
  secret nuclear weapon
    programme 153 n.8
British Labour Party 86
Brown, G. W. 6

Calhoun, C. 4, 7
Campbell, J. 13 n.5
capitalism 10, 51–2, 75, 83, 89, 115–16
  American capitalism 2, 75
  American corporate capitalism 2, 46, 95
  consumer capitalism 65
  corporate capitalism 2, 46, 95
  hegemonic identification of 67
  hegemony of 71
  palliative measures 71
  profit system of 86, 89
  twentieth-century capitalism 138 n.4
  welfare state capitalism 142 n.4
capitalist economy 95, 99, 118
capitalist social order 75
Caspary, W. R. 136 n.17, 137–8 n.1
centralized federal government 57
Chandler, D. 123
Chang, H. J. 8, 132 n.2
China 3, 122
citizenship rights 7
Civil Rights Act 132 n.1
Civil Rights Movement 1
climate change 9, 96, 123–4, 129
Cochran, M. 3, 6, 113, 119–21, 139, 140 n.10, 151 n.4
cogs 62
communications technology 2, 42, 104
communism 3, 18, 88
  opposition of 142 n.5

communist utopia 39
comparative advantage theory 131 n.3
comprehensive unemployment insurance 69
conflict resolution 136 n.17
conflicts 31, 36, 65
consumer capitalism
  hegemony of 65
  perpetuation of 65
consumer culture, elements of 66
corporate structure, revolution 17
cosmopolitanism
  collapse of the 152 n.6
  Eurocentrism of 7
  failings of 7
  modern cosmopolitanism 6–7
  pragmatic cosmopolitanism 152 n.7
  rooted 12, 104, 112, 120–1, 125
Council for a Democratic Germany 121
creative democracy
  arresting of 57
  breakdown of 73, 116
  definitive blueprints 76
  global level views 51
  ideals of 72
  international form of 111
  within local community 110
  national and global eclipse of 66–73
  political democracy 37
  social and humane 60
  stunting of 11, 60, 70
  through social intelligence 12, 83, 96, 99, 110
  vitality of 112
cultural freedom 86, 95
cultural and institutional lag 144 n.7
cultural matrix 21–3, 25–8, 31–2, 80–1, 94
  changes in 25
  conception of 133 n.8
  consequences of associated behaviour 26

historical propensity 25
industrial/capitalist-based
  societies 134 n.11
intellectual foundations 28
material aspects 135 n.13
perceptions of consequences 26
perpetual propensity 27
variety of associations 26
cultural politics, valorization of
  137 n.20
cultural subjugation 100

Dale, G. 153 n.8
Darwin, Charles 20
Deen, P. 95–7, 146 n.9
de-globalisation 138 n.3
democracy
  apparent failure of 66
  attacks by communism 18
  bourgeois democracy 11–12
  equality and 88–95
  global inheritance of 53
  hegemonic identification of 67
  national 5, 9–10, 117, 124–5
  political democracy 37
  problematizations of 128
  radical faith in 125
  reform of 53
  teleological advance of 49
  way of life 31–6
    conception of democracy 32
    co-operative problem-solving
      36
    democratic realism 31
    ethical commitment 13, 33,
      35, 37, 78, 89, 97, 108,
      137 n.19, 149
    ideal or idea 32
    political democracy 32
democracy at home
  achievement of 76, 103
  crisis of 124
  cultural reorganization of 18
  eclipse of 54
  emergence of 129

  form of 112
  international arena 97
  linked with democracy abroad
    114, 116, 129–30
  perpetuation of 144 n.6
  persistence 123
  political 117
  problem of 104, 120, 129
  renewal of 118
  roots of 120
  use of 104
  vitality of 114
democratic disillusionment 125
democratic globalization 4–9
democratic governance 56, 122
democratic inheritance 129–30
democratic liberty, conception of 91
democratic politics, fighting faith of
  130
democratic realism 10, 15–16, 18–19,
  31, 46, 57–8, 62, 65, 132 n.4
  in America 19
  charge of 16
  fascism, and 18
  governance of 142
  opposition 31
  quasi-Platonism 18
  rise of 46
  superficial agreement with 57
democratic socialism 12, 77, 86–9,
  94, 116
  form of 76–7, 92, 98, 116
  national form of 112
  and political economy 89
distributive justice, principles of
  146 n.9
Dryzek, J. 5, 7, 124, 139 n.5
Duménil, G. 131 n.3

Eckerlsey, R. 151 n.5
eclipse of the public 57–66
  in America 76
  cultural and structural
    inequalities 116
  effects of 66

intellectual deficiency 65
intelligence of masses 61
　perpetuation of 67
　political effect of the 68
ecological democracy 148 n.12
economic inequality 59, 61, 66, 77, 92–3, 96, 144 n.6
effective intelligence 61, 84, 100
efficient market hypothesis 131 n.3
egalitarianism 12, 77, 116
Eldridge, M. 75, 142 n.1
embedded liberal states 154 n.10
employment 59
Englen, E. 122
environmental democracy 148 n.12
equality
　economic equality 12, 89, 92–3, 95, 99, 101, 103, 146 n.8
　equality between nations 98
　ethical commitment of democracy 89
　freedom of information 96
　global climate change 96
　global distributive justice 100
　gross economic inequality 96
　human rights 96
　of labour standards 98
　philosophical liberalism 97
　political equality 12, 89, 91, 93
　rights of expression 96
　of trade conditions 99
　women's equality 26
Escobar, A. 7
European Central Bank 124
European democracy, collapse of 76
European imperialism 1, 42
Eurozone crisis 124
evolution theory 50. *See also* Darwin, Charles
exceptionalism 146 n.10

Farmer-Labour Political Federation (FLPF) 88
fascism 3, 18, 71–3, 78
　opposition of 142 n.5

finance-capitalism 59, 92–3
　hegemony of 85, 122
financial crisis, aftermath of 123
Findlay, R. 42–4, 138 n.1–2
Fine, R. 4
First Great Globalization 9, 11, 41–3, 45–6, 49, 95
　de-globalization period 44
　global migration 42
　Great Society as 42–5
　industrial revolution 42
　internationalization of commercial banks 45
　opening up of Asia to free trade 42
　radical transformation 42
　re-establishment of gold standard 44
　rise of trade protectionism 44
　trade growth 43
First World War 3, 9, 15–16, 44, 47–8, 70, 98
　aftermath of the destruction 51
folly of masses 18
Fordism, mass-production techniques 62
foreign currencies, depreciations of 47
foreign direct investment 45
Frankfurt School 75
free trade 42, 57, 97–8, 115
Frieden, J. A. 16–17, 42–3, 45, 131 n.3, 132 n.3, 154 n.10

Germany 15, 47–8, 114
　hyperinflation 48
Gilded Age 2, 75
Gilens, M. 123
global democracy 1, 6–13, 41, 51–3, 55–7, 70, 73, 103–4, 107–10, 112, 114–26, 129
　active part of 109
　appraisal of 121
　basic provision of 71
　collapse of 10

difficulty in creating 56
difficulty facing 73
equality 95–101
   freedom of information 96
   global climate change 96
   global distributive justice 100
   gross economic inequality 96
   human rights 96
   labour standards 98
   rights of expression 96
   trade conditions 99
fullest expression 120
future of 72
key focal points of 109
modern ideas about 104
nation state as a key vehicle 117
nature of 103
optimism towards the 56
overarching blueprints of 51
post-Westphalian 7–8, 120
potential for 106
problematizing of 103
statist approach 120
theorizations of 119
top-down pathways to 6
transitory stages in 107
two-pronged approach 51
global governance, forms of 8
global governance (UN) institutions 7
global inequality 8, 129
global interdependence 97–8
globalization. *See also* First Great Globalization
   dating of 138 n.2
   economic 49, 121, 136 n.17
   effects of 54
   fate of democracy 4
   modern 49, 131 n.2
   nature of 55
   neo-liberal 5, 8, 9, 121–2, 130, 131 n.3, 143 n.1
   problematizations of 128
   reality of 48
   relation with democracy 4
   rise of 9

global justice, minimalist conceptions 146 n.9
global multilateralism 124
glorious revolution of 1688 90
gold reserves, centralization of 47
gold standards 42
Gouinlock, J. 22, 82, 134 n.9, 143 n.4–5, 147 n.12
Great Community
   colonial possessions 47
   creation of 11, 106
   emergence of 49, 56–7, 95
   forming issues 106–7, 110, 117
   international associative relationships 105
   international form 70, 99, 111
   nation and 106–9
   racial and cultural differences 47
   social intelligence within 128, 146 n.9
   technological advancements 105
Great Depression 3, 44–5, 49, 56, 59, 63, 73, 90
   material inequality 59
   onset of 141 n.1
   political activism 87
   trade protectionism 44, 73
Great Recession 122
Great Society
   associative relationships 105
   complexity 73, 112
   concept of 16
   consequences of 68–9, 71
   consequences engendered by 73
   cultural freedom 95
   economic equality 12
   economic reorganization of 91
   emergence of 17, 77
   engendering of divided and troubled publics 73
   ethical commitment 94
   global conditions 111
   global dimensions of 11, 41, 45
   globalization and 128
   global nature of 47–8, 53

industrial and economic relations 62
international associative relationships 105
international effects of 49–50
irony of 69
manoeuvrings of the 58
national associations 56
national conditions of 111
nature of 41, 63
political equality 12
political ideals 78
problem of democracy 19
regulation of 111
scientific revolutions and 128
social effects of 68
technological advancements 105, 108
transnational associations 56
transnational consequences 72
transnational nature of 73, 112
transnational reality of 50
world nations interdependence 106

Habermas, J. 5–7, 123, 139 n.5, 141 n.3, 143 n.3
habits
of belief 50
conflicting 22
consequences of 24
democratic 76, 79, 85–7, 89, 99, 110, 128–9
diffusion of 146 n.8
intellectual 25
personal moral 21
quasi-democratic 65
scientific attitude 85
social habits 61
social intelligence 77–84, 91, 99, 110, 150 n.13
of thought 106
Hale, T. 7, 9, 123
Hardt, M. 5, 7, 150 n.1

Harvey, D. 131 n.3, 142 n.4, 154 n.10
Hay, C. 121–2, 144 n.6
Heidegger, M. 2
Held, D. 5–6, 139 n.5
Hickman, L 137–8 n.1
Hirst, P. 121–2
historical relativity of culture 31, 36
Hobbes, Thomas 5
Hobson, J. M. 7
homosexuals/homosexuality 26, 29
Honneth, A. 133 n.5, 143 n.3, 144 n.5, 145 n.8
Hopkins, A. G. 138 n.2
Horkheimer, M. 75
hyperinflation 44, 48

IMF 5, 122, 124
immigrants 29
immigration 26, 51
imperialism 43–4, 51, 98–9, 113, 115
economic 152 n.6
European imperialism 1, 42
political 152 n.6
shackles of 71
income inequality 125
India 122
individuality 133 n.6
industrial complexity, rise of 9
industrial democracy 59, 142 n.4
industrial revolution 16–17, 42, 138
first 16
second 16
industrial tariffs, problem of 58
industrial-technological revolution 46, 77–8, 83, 92–3, 95, 150 n.1
inequality 85
institutionalizing of revolution 39
intellectual hypocrisy 59
intellectual inequality 66
intercontinental trade system 42
International Chaos 139 n.6
International Co-operation 139 n.6
international order, reformation of 53
isolationism 71

James, William 2, 20
Japan 43, 47

Kadlec, A. 46, 133 n.5, 137–8 n.1, 143 n.3
Kaldor, M. 7
Katz, E. 148 n.12
Keck, M. 121
Kennedy, P. 16
Keynes, J. M. 43–4, 138 n.4
Kloppenberg, J. T. 15
Koopman, C. 144 n.6, 148–9 n.13
Kymlicka, W. 150 n.1

laissez-faire capitalism 60–1, 90
　conception of liberty 61
　defenders of 65
　democratic realism and 61
　hegemony of 61, 63, 68
　human liberty 60
　ideal of 90
　individualism 90–1
　liberty 90–1
　merits of 63
　strictures of 61
laissez-faire liberalism 92, 95, 144 n.7
　social consequences of 92
League of Free Nations 121
League for Independent Political Action (LIPA) 88, 143 n.2
League of Nations 52, 98, 109, 140 n.10
Leuchtenburg, W. 17, 140–1 n.1
Lévy, D. 131 n.3
liberal capitalism 12, 51, 76–7, 99, 115–16, 123, 145 n.8, 147 n.12
　doctrine of 115
　fundamental reorganization of 116
　hegemony of 123
　hegemony of the tenets of 116
　incompatibility of 117
　tenets of 99
liberal democracy 7
　gain for the masses within 59

liberal democratic governments, historic emergence 59
liberalism
　democratic political 91
　economic 59, 123, 154 n.10
　failure of modern proponents of 61
　philosophical 60, 90, 97
　pseudo-liberalism 90
　reconstruction of 89, 92
Liberalism and Social Action 3–4, 89
liberty
　democratic conception of 93
　democratic distribution of 91–2, 94–5, 99–100
　economic-liberty 147
　historical relativity of 90
　human liberty 60
　individualism and 90
　philosophical liberalism 97
　philosophy of liberty 61
　reconstruction of 89
Light, A. 148 n.12
Lind, M. 16, 132 n.2
Lippmann, W. 10, 16–19, 58
Livingston, J. 137 n.20, 141 n.1, 144 n.6, 146 n.8
local community 110–12
localism 111
Lukacs, G. 75

Martin, J. 4, 143 n.2
Marxist-style conspiracy 135 n.15
mass communication revolution 105
mass consumption, revolution of 17
material culture 26
material inequality 85, 98
Mazower, M. 123, 153 n.9
McDermott, J. 103, 144 n.5
McGrew, A. 5
Mead, G. H. 39
Mein Kampf 15
mercantilism 60
military forms of warfare 49

military technologies, advancement of 136 n.16
Mills, C. W. 75
modern sovereignty 5, 10, 106, 121
  collapse/decline of 5, 10, 107
  parameters of declining 109
moral conflicts 32, 34, 36, 82
Morris, I. 16
Mosley, L. 121
multipolarity 123–4
Mumford, L. 2, 75

Nagel, T. 146 n.9
Napoleonic Wars 108
National Association for the Advancement of Colored People (NAACP) 143 n.2
nationalism
  aggressive side of 108
  anti-cosmopolitan 116
  bullheaded 107
  cosmopolitan 151 n.5
  cultural 152 n.7
  European 48, 107
  exacerbated Nationalism 72
  form of 108
  hyper-nationalism 72
  muscular 140
  as positive advance 108
  pull of 113
  Third World nationalism 147 n.11, 150 n.2
  two-sided 108
  xenophobic nationalism 44
nationalization of industries 86
national sovereignty 107
nation state
  American 42, 70, 115
  autonomous 5
  community sense 57
  counterparts 6
  creative democracy 57, 66, 71, 73, 112
  democracy reforms 53
  democratic praxis 126
  disharmony 68
  eclipse of public 68, 72
  emergence of 151 n.3
  European citizens 124
  habits of social intelligence 115
  importance of 120
  intellectual inequality 116
  interdependence in Great Society 48
  as a key vehicle 117
  material inequality 116
  modern conceptions 134 n.10
  naked power of 109
  outdated policies of 107
  persistence of 121
  political democracy 67
  political fusion 107
  political standing 99
  re-emergence of publics 118
  relations with publics 51
  role of 104, 109, 139 n.5
  stagnation of political democracy 123
  status of 5
  troubled publics 72
Negri, A. 5, 7, 150 n.1
neo-imperialism, Western nations 152 n.6
neo-liberal globalization 5, 7–9, 121, 130–1
  deterritorialization of political authority 5
  midst of 143 n.1
  policy recommendations of 131 n.3
  primary effect of 5
  ramifications of 5
neo-liberal imperatives 5
neo-liberalism 1, 4
  hegemony of 122, 124
  rise of 122
New Deal era 87
New World Slavery 29
non-whites 29
North/South relations 51

Occupy Movement 7
October Revolution 15
old diplomacy, aristocratic style 52
Origin of the Species 1
O'Rourke, K. H. 42–4, 138 n.2–3
Outlawry for War Movement 121

Pappas, G. F. 142 n.1, 143 n.4,
    144 n.5, 147 n.12
participatory democracy 87
Patomäki, H. 7
Pax Romana 48
pecuniary profit system 65
People's Lobby (PL) 88, 143 n.2
Phantom Public, The 16
philosophical pragmatism 2, 95
Pierce, Charles Sanders 2
planning society 85–8
pluralist philosophy 28
Polanyi, Karl 153 n.8
political democracy
    elements of 7
    outcome of 68
    pincer effect 67
    political malaise 67
    stagnation of 123
political philosophy 3–4, 9, 11, 19
political responsibility 54, 107, 113
political settlement 15, 28, 31, 34, 39,
    78, 82–3
poll taxes 132 n.1
post-democratic bureaucratic rule
    124
post-war social democracy, collapse
    of 122
post-Westphalian global democracy
    6–8, 103–4, 119
    advocates of 123
    clamour for 123
    failings of 125
pragmatic democracy 148 n.13
pragmatism 2, 75, 95–6
Prashad, V. 131 n.3, 152 n.6, 153 n.9
privileged plutocracy 117
problematic states 19–28

problem-solving, co-operative 36, 69
protectionism 57, 107
Public and Its Problems, The 3, 9–11,
    15, 19, 45–7, 53, 56, 70–1
Public Opinion 16
public(s)
    ability of 137 n.20
    bottom-up processes of 119
    communicative inclusion of 35
    conflicts 39
    definitions 25–8
    diachronic level 26
    divided and troubled 56, 72–3
    eclipsed 57–8, 73, 125
    emergence of 27, 31
    fall of 37
    functional logic 28
    historical relativity of 36
    history of 28–31
    illiberal 29
    interests of 135 n.14
    newly formed 30
    political efficacy of 126
    problems of 45
    progressive 29
    propriety or reasonableness 28
    re-emergence of 118
    resistance organized 136 n.16
    rise of 28, 37
    synchronically and diachronically
        27
    transnational leaders of 113
Putnam, H. 143 n.3, 144 n.5

racist-inspired literacy tests 132 n.1
racist segregation 59
radical democratic tradition 2
radical third party 88
Ralston, S. J. 148 n.12
Rao, R. 7
Rawls, J. 146 n.9, 148–9 n.13
reasonable pluralism 148
reformed education 69
regressive income tax 59
revolutionary violence 136 n.16

Rodrik, D. 8, 42–3, 122, 138 n.2, 154 n.10
rooted cosmopolitism 118
Rorty, R. 3, 88, 131–2 n.4
rugged individualism 61, 70, 93
Ruggie, J. G. 142 n.4, 154 n.10
Russell, B. 2, 75
Ryan, A. 151 n.4

Scholte, J. 6–7
Second World War 3, 49–50, 55–6, 99
   destructiveness of 49
   developments after 53
   old-time diplomacy 50
   rise of atomic age 50
semi-socialist market economy 88
Sen, J. 7
sensationalism 65
Siamese' twins 67
Sikkink, K. 121
slave-based agrarian economy 16
Smith, J. 125
Smith, W. 7
social contract theory 20
Social Democratic Parties of Europe 86
social institutions, reform of 66, 68
social intelligence
   appraisal of moral conflict 82
   attitude of the mind 79
   in the context of Great Society 92
   co-operative inquiry 83
   cultural matrix and social policy 80
   deliberation within the democratic community 81
   democratic habits of 85–6, 99, 115
   experimental method of 79, 80
   habits of 77–84, 91, 99, 106, 110, 114, 118
   justification for democracy 144 n.5
   moral and political conflict 82
   moral relativism 80
   national form of 112
   nature of 143 n.5
   non-absolutism of 82
   organised application of 83
   reflective morality 80
   remit of 81
   role of 79
social policy
   formation of 33
   participation and communication 33
Spanish-American War 3
spatial globalism 7
state activism 135 n.14
state socialism 86
state theory
   futility of 19–28
   political instincts 19
   state-forming forces 19
Stiglitz, J. E. 122
stratification, intellectual hegemony 63
structural inequality 145 n.8
swing-style democracy 67

Talisse, R. B. 148 n.13
Tan, K. C. 151 n.5
Tarrow, S. 112, 121–2
technological advancements 105, 108
theory of psychology 20. *See also* James, William
Third Reich 39
totalitarianism 72, 76, 78, 113
town-meeting 111
trade protectionism 44, 49
transactions, private and public 23–4
transnational activism 112, 121
Treaty of Westphalia 5
triviality 65
Trotsky, Leon 3
Truman Doctrine 3
Turkey 3, 47
two-party adversarial politics 70

United Nations 6, 54, 122
United States
   depreciations of foreign currencies 47

economic output 16
political isolationism 45
re-establishment of gold standard 44
rejected Britain's political engagement 44
struggle against Soviet Union 3

Vietnam War 1
violent revolution 10, 30–1, 35
    catalyst for 30–1
völksgemeinschaft 72
Voting Rights Act 132 n.1

Wade, R. 8, 122–3, 154 n.11
Wallas, G. 16
war debts 47
wealth inequality 122
wealth redistribution 86

Weiss, L. 122
welfare states 154 n.10
Westbrook, R. 2–3, 13, 15–16, 46, 75, 87–8, 91, 99, 132 n.4, 134 n.12, 135 n.14, 137 n.1, 138 n.1, 140 n.10, 142 n.1, 142 n.5, 143 n.3, 144 n.5–6, 151 n.4
West, C. 75, 131 n.3, 150 n.1, 154 n.11
women's equality 26
workplace democracy 69, 87
World Bank 5, 122
World Social Forum 7
Wu, T. 141 n.3

xenophobia 125
xenophobic nationalism 44

Zapatistas movement 7

EU authorised representative for GPSR:
Easy Access System Europe, Mustamäe tee 50,
10621 Tallinn, Estonia
gpsr.requests@easproject.com

www.ingramcontent.com/pod-product-compliance
Ingram Content Group UK Ltd.
Pitfield, Milton Keynes, MK11 3LW, UK
UKHW021841140426
5217IPUK00022B/1539